With God She Rises

A Daily Journal for Christian Mompreneurs

By Stefanie Gass

Fear not, for I am
with you; be not
dismayed, for I am
your God; I will
strengthen you, I will
help you, I will uphold
you with my
righteous right hand.

Isaiah 41:10

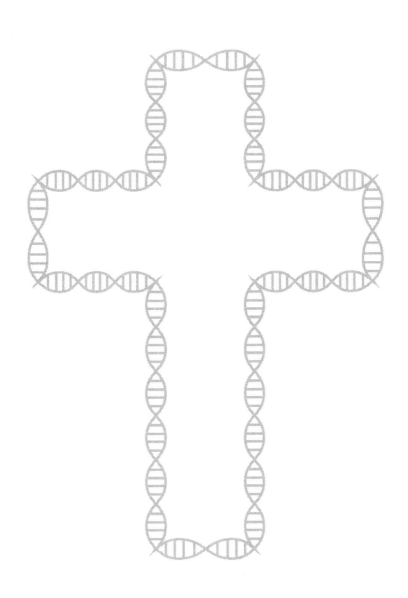

I pray over you mama, that your life is fueled by God's grace, love, provision, and prosperity. I pray that you pour into your gifts and uncover the potential that lies within your heart. I pray that God covers you in strength. Not only an exceptional, patient, and kind mama, but also a world changer. I am cheering for you. In his glorious name, Amen.

For God gave us a
spirit not of fear but
of power and love and
self—control.

2 Timothy 1:7

This journal can change your life.

For the past 6 years, I have been using the tools and routines from this book to create my best, God-fueled life. From running very successful businesses to being an exceptional wife and mama, to loving myself, fully and unconditionally.

With God, I have risen.

You too, can step into your own potential and claim the life of your dreams. Take the time to use your journal, both morning and night. Set a reminder. If you skip a day, just pick up where you left off. Be sure to fill out the miracles and holy spirit moments every time you see or feel God move in your life. These moments are worth remembering! Write out your 1 and 5-year vision statements in the present tense and be as descriptive as possible! You want to describe a day in your dream life. Create tangible goals that will allow your vision to become a reality.

I am cheering for you.

Love and Light,
Stef Gass

HOW HAS GOD MOVED IN YOUR LIFE RECENTLY?

Take note of the miracles and provision that God provides. Every miracle deserves to be remembered, and shared!

Miracles & Holy Spirit Moments

Miracles & Holy Spirit Moments

Miracles & Holy Spirit Moments

Three things will last forever—faith, hope, and love—and the greatest of these is love.

1 Corinthians 13:13

what life categories do you need in order to fill your cup? what amount of time needs to be spent in each life category? Doing what?

Spiritual

Self-Care

Family

Health / Fitness

Business

Other

For it is by grace you
have been
saved, through faith—
and this is not from
yourselves, it is the
gift of God.

Ephesians 2:8

Begin by imagining your life 5 years from now.

Think about what you really want. How would your life feel? What would your finances look like? Imagine your family and where they will be 5 years from today. What will your relationships be like? What about your business and your health? What will your relationship with God be like?

Don't put a limit on your dream life.

This exercise is limitless. You know no boundaries. Next, write out a day in your dream life, 5 years from today. Take into account all of the questions I have listed above. Go into detail in every aspect. Be descriptive. Create the vision so you can feel it and visualize it clearly.

After you're done, follow the same exercise 1 year from today. Your 1-year vision is a stepping stone to creating your dream life, 5 years from now. Use these vision statements to create tangible goals and action items that will move you forward.

Five Year Vision Statement

Five Year Vision Statement

One Year Vision Statement

One Year Vision Statement

12 Month Goal Mapping
what 10 things need to happen in order for my 1-year vision to become a Reality?

10 Tangible & Specific Annual Goals

1.
2.
3.
4.
5.
6.
7.
8.
9.
10.

Monthly Goal Mapping
what needs to happen each month to achieve your annual goals?

Tangible & Specific
Monthly Goals

1
2
3
4
5
6
7
8
9
10

Weekly Goal Mapping
What needs to happen each week to achieve your monthly goals?

Tangible & Specific
Weekly Goals

1
2
3
4
5
6
7
8
9
10

Ideas :: Inspiration :: Notes

I am strong. I am brave. I am loved. I am favored. I welcome God's provision and guidance today, and everyday.

Date

Lord God, today I pray for

I am grateful for...

Today, I choose to feel

My personal goals for today

My business goals for today

Breathe. God's got this. Trust Him!

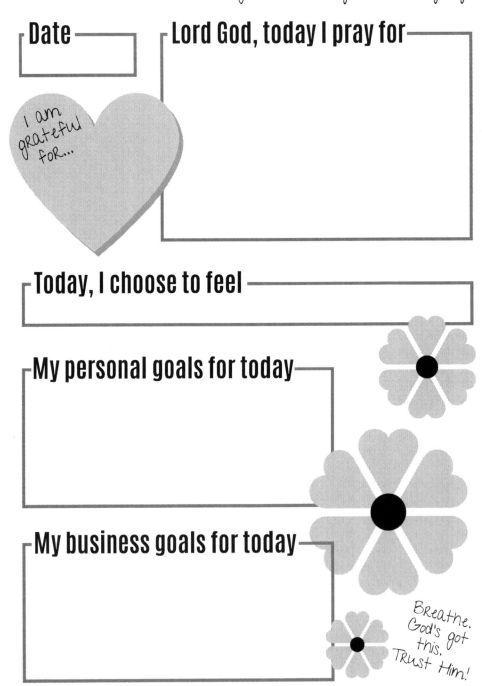

GOOD NIGHT EMPOWERED MAMA

I am grateful for a life full of God's infinite blessings. My heart is open to what's next. I trust Him.

Lord God, thank you for

my favorite moment/memory from today was

Today, I felt

I achieved my personal goals | Yes :: No
I achieved my business goals | Yes :: No

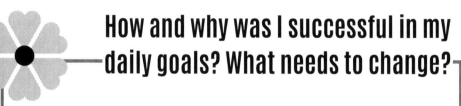

How and why was I successful in my daily goals? What needs to change?

I trust in God's timing. Relax. Breathe. Rest.

I am stRoNg. I am bRave. I am loved. I am favoRed. I welcome God's pRovision and guidance today, and everyday.

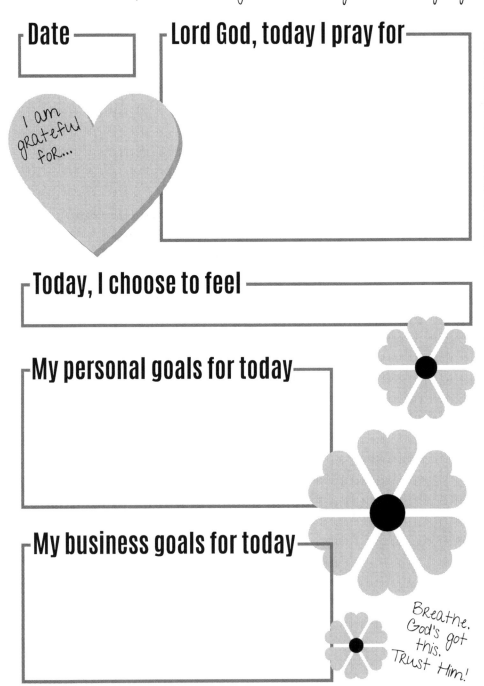

Date

Lord God, today I pray for

I am gRateful foR...

Today, I choose to feel

My personal goals for today

My business goals for today

BReathe. God's got this. TRust Him!

am grateful for a life full of God's infinite blessings. My heart is open to what's next. I trust Him.

Lord God, thank you for

my favorite moment/memory from today was

Today, I felt

I achieved my personal goals | Yes :: No
I achieved my business goals | Yes :: No

How and why was I successful in my daily goals? What needs to change?

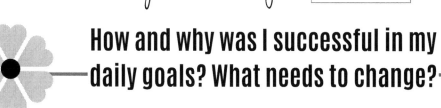

I Trust in God's timing. Relax. Breathe. Rest.

I am strong. I am brave. I am loved. I am favored. I welcome God's provision and guidance today, and everyday.

Date

Lord God, today I pray for

I am grateful for...

Today, I choose to feel

My personal goals for today

My business goals for today

Breathe. God's got this. Trust Him!

I am grateful for a life full of God's infinite blessings. My heart is open to what's next. I trust Him.

Lord God, thank you for

my favorite moment/memory from today was

Today, I felt

I achieved my personal goals | Yes :: No
I achieved my business goals | Yes :: No

How and why was I successful in my daily goals? What needs to change?

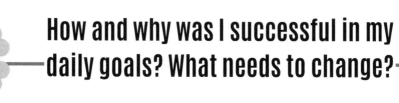

I Trust in God's timing. Relax. Breathe. Rest.

I am stRong. I am bRave. I am loved. I am favoRed. I welcome God's pRovision and guidance today, and everyday.

Date

Lord God, today I pray for

I am gRateful foR...

Today, I choose to feel

My personal goals for today

My business goals for today

Breathe. God's got this. TRust Him!

am grateful for a life full of God's infinite blessings. my heart is open to what's next. I trust Him.

Lord God, thank you for

my favorite moment/memory from today was

Today, I felt

I achieved my personal goals | Yes :: No
I achieved my business goals | Yes :: No

How and why was I successful in my daily goals? What needs to change?

Trust in God's timing. Relax. Breathe. Rest.

I am stRONG. I am bRave. I am loved. I am favoRed. I welcome God's pRovision and guidance today, and everyday.

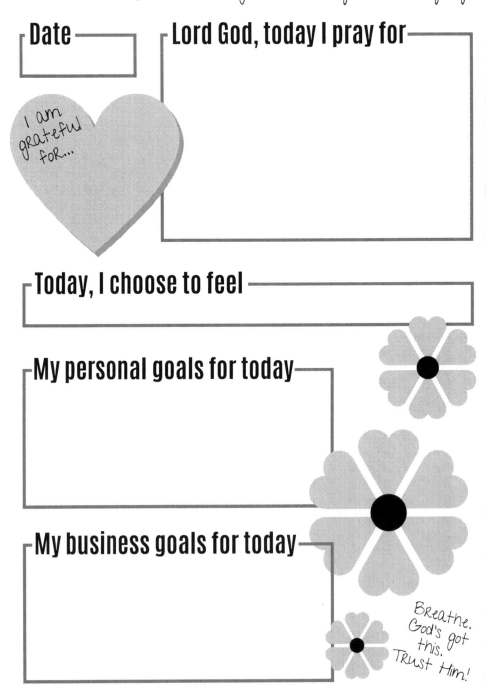

Date

Lord God, today I pray for

I am grateful foR...

Today, I choose to feel

My personal goals for today

My business goals for today

Breathe. God's got this. TRust Him!

GOOD NIGHT EMPOWERED MAMA

am grateful for a life full of God's infinite blessings. My heart is open to what's next. I trust Him.

Lord God, thank you for

my favorite moment/memory from today was

Today, I felt

I achieved my personal goals | Yes :: No
I achieved my business goals | Yes :: No

How and why was I successful in my daily goals? What needs to change?

Trust in God's timing. Relax. Breathe. Rest.

I am stRoNG. I am bRave. I am loved. I am favoRed. I welcome God's pRovision and guidance today, and everyday.

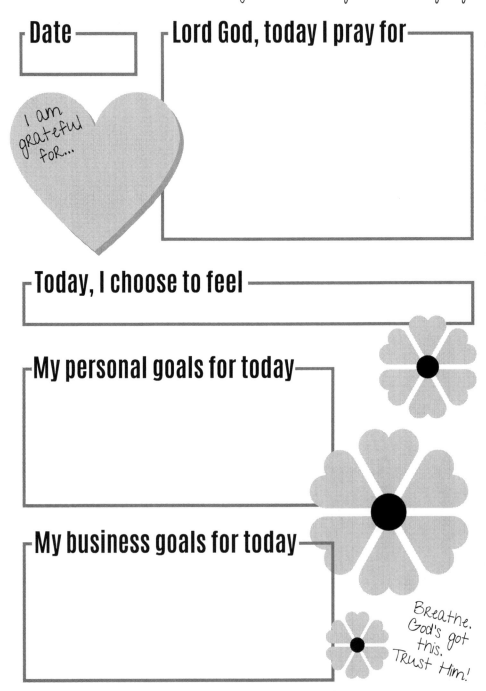

Date

Lord God, today I pray for

I am gRateful foR...

Today, I choose to feel

My personal goals for today

My business goals for today

BReathe. God's got this. TRust Him!

am grateful for a life full of God's infinite blessings. My heart is open to what's next. I trust Him.

Lord God, thank you for

my favorite moment/memory from today was

Today, I felt

I achieved my personal goals — Yes :: No
I achieved my business goals — Yes :: No

How and why was I successful in my daily goals? What needs to change?

I trust in God's timing. Relax. Breathe. Rest.

I am stRoNg. I am bRave. I am loved. I am favoReD. I welcome God's pRovision and guidance today, and everyday.

Date

Lord God, today I pray for

I am gRateful foR...

Today, I choose to feel

My personal goals for today

My business goals for today

BReathe. God's got this. Trust Him!

I am grateful for a life full of God's infinite blessings. My heart is open to what's next. I trust Him.

Lord God, thank you for

my favorite moment/memory from today was

Today, I felt

I achieved my personal goals | Yes :: No

I achieved my business goals | Yes :: No

How and why was I successful in my daily goals? What needs to change?

I trust in God's timing. Relax. Breathe. Rest.

I am strong. I am brave. I am loved. I am favored. I welcome God's provision and guidance today, and everyday.

Date

Lord God, today I pray for

I am grateful for...

Today, I choose to feel

My personal goals for today

My business goals for today

Breathe. God's got this. Trust Him!

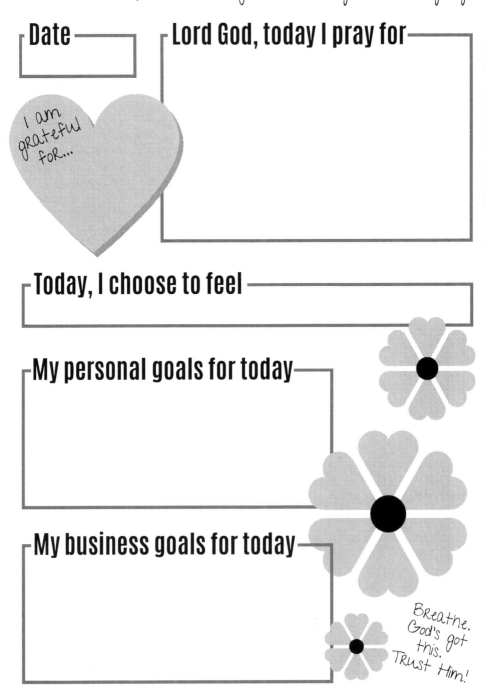

am grateful for a life full of God's infinite blessings. My heart is open to what's next. I trust Him.

Lord God, thank you for

my favorite moment/memory from today was

Today, I felt

I achieved my personal goals | Yes :: No

I achieved my business goals | Yes :: No

How and why was I successful in my daily goals? What needs to change?

I trust in God's timing. Relax. Breathe. Rest.

I am strong. I am brave. I am loved. I am favored. I welcome God's provision and guidance today, and everyday.

Date

Lord God, today I pray for

I am grateful for...

Today, I choose to feel

My personal goals for today

My business goals for today

Breathe. God's got this. Trust Him!

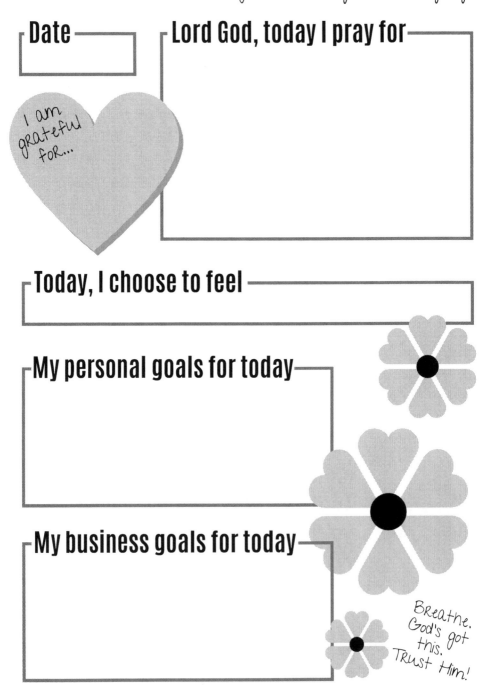

am grateful for a life full of God's infinite blessings. My heart is open to what's next. I trust Him.

Lord God, thank you for

my favorite moment/memory from today was

Today, I felt

I achieved my personal goals | **Yes :: No**
I achieved my business goals | **Yes :: No**

How and why was I successful in my daily goals? What needs to change?

I trust in God's timing. Relax. Breathe. Rest.

I am strong. I am brave. I am loved. I am favored. I welcome God's provision and guidance today, and everyday.

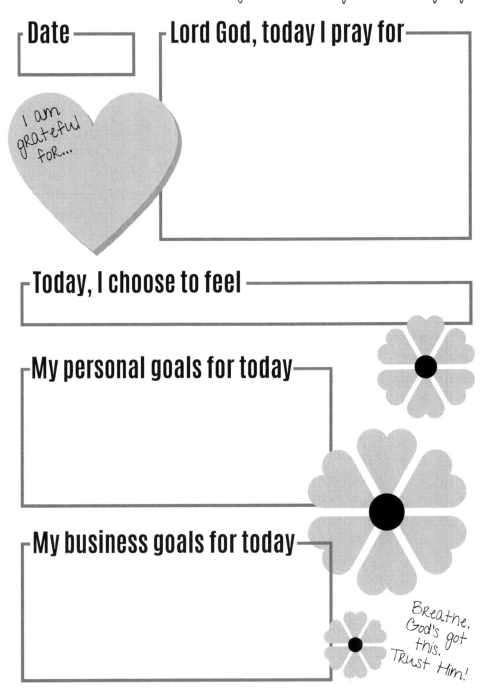

Date

Lord God, today I pray for

I am grateful for...

Today, I choose to feel

My personal goals for today

My business goals for today

Breathe. God's got this. Trust Him!

I am grateful for a life full of God's infinite blessings. My heart is open to what's next. I trust Him.

Lord God, thank you for

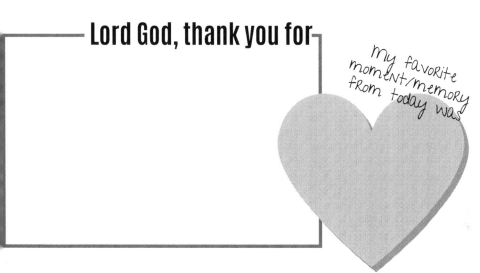

my favorite moment/memory from today was

Today, I felt

I achieved my personal goals | Yes :: No

I achieved my business goals | Yes :: No

How and why was I successful in my daily goals? What needs to change?

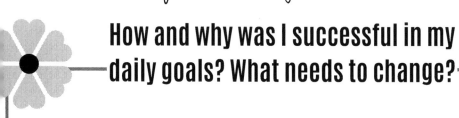

I Trust in God's timing. Relax. Breathe. Rest.

I am strong. I am brave. I am loved. I am favored. I welcome God's provision and guidance today, and everyday.

Date

Lord God, today I pray for

I am grateful for....

Today, I choose to feel

My personal goals for today

My business goals for today

Breathe. God's got this. Trust Him!

am grateful for a life full of God's infinite blessings. My heart is open to what's next. I trust Him.

Lord God, thank you for

my favorite moment/memory from today was

Today, I felt

I achieved my personal goals | Yes :: No
I achieved my business goals | Yes :: No

How and why was I successful in my daily goals? What needs to change?

Trust in God's timing. Relax. Breathe. Rest.

I am strong. I am brave. I am loved. I am favored. I welcome God's provision and guidance today, and everyday.

Date

I am grateful for...

Lord God, today I pray for

Today, I choose to feel

My personal goals for today

My business goals for today

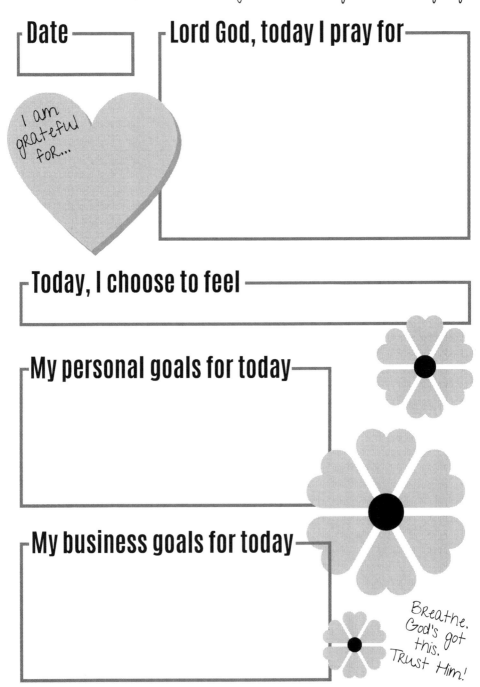

Breathe. God's got this. Trust Him!

am grateful for a life full of God's infinite blessings. My
heart is open to what's next. I trust Him.

Lord God, thank you for

my favorite
moment/memory
from today was

Today, I felt

I achieved my personal goals | Yes :: No
I achieved my business goals | Yes :: No

How and why was I successful in my daily goals? What needs to change?

I trust in God's timing. Relax. Breathe. Rest.

I am strong. I am brave. I am loved. I am favored. I welcome God's provision and guidance today, and everyday.

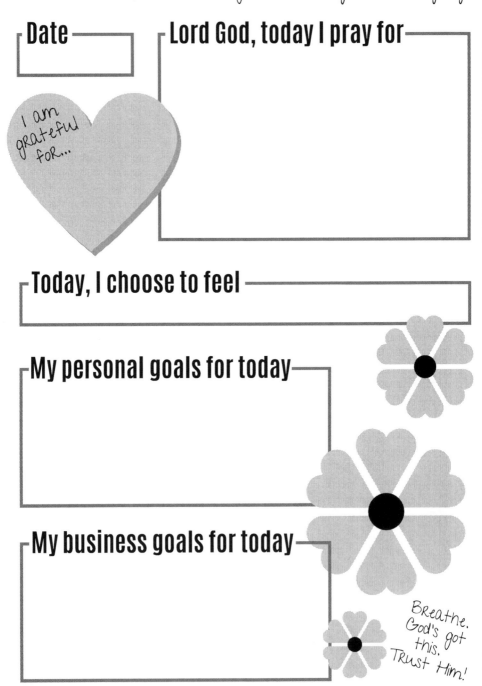

Date

Lord God, today I pray for

I am grateful for...

Today, I choose to feel

My personal goals for today

My business goals for today

Breathe. God's got this. Trust Him!

am grateful for a life full of God's infinite blessings. My heart is open to what's next. I trust Him.

Lord God, thank you for

my favorite moment/memory from today was

Today, I felt

I achieved my personal goals Yes :: No
I achieved my business goals Yes :: No

How and why was I successful in my daily goals? What needs to change?

Trust in God's timing. Relax. Breathe. Rest.

I am strong. I am brave. I am loved. I am favored. I welcome God's provision and guidance today, and everyday.

Date

Lord God, today I pray for

I am grateful for...

Today, I choose to feel

My personal goals for today

My business goals for today

Breathe. God's got this. Trust Him!

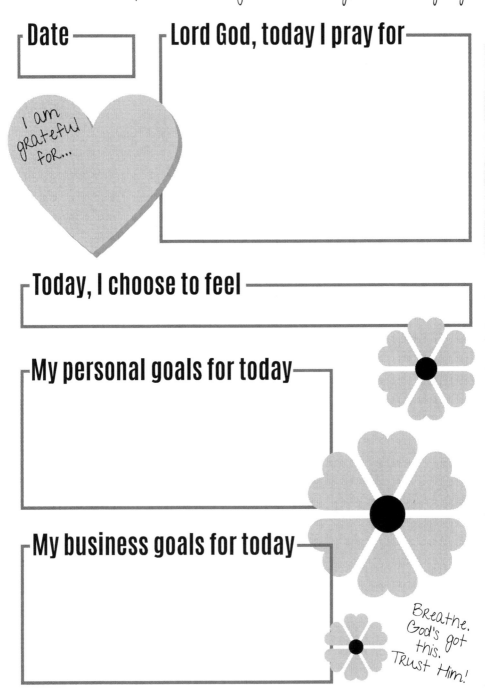

am grateful for a life full of God's infinite blessings. My heart is open to what's next. I trust Him.

Lord God, thank you for

my favorite moment/memory from today was

Today, I felt

I achieved my personal goals | Yes :: No

I achieved my business goals | Yes :: No

How and why was I successful in my daily goals? What needs to change?

Trust in God's timing. Relax. Breathe. Rest.

I am strong. I am brave. I am loved. I am favored. I welcome God's provision and guidance today, and everyday.

Date

Lord God, today I pray for

I am grateful for...

Today, I choose to feel

My personal goals for today

My business goals for today

Breathe. God's got this. Trust Him!

am grateful for a life full of God's infinite blessings. My heart is open to what's next. I trust Him.

Lord God, thank you for

my favorite moment/memory from today was

Today, I felt

I achieved my personal goals | Yes :: No
I achieved my business goals | Yes :: No

How and why was I successful in my daily goals? What needs to change?

I Trust in God's timing. Relax. Breathe. Rest.

I am strong. I am brave. I am loved. I am favored. I welcome God's provision and guidance today, and everyday.

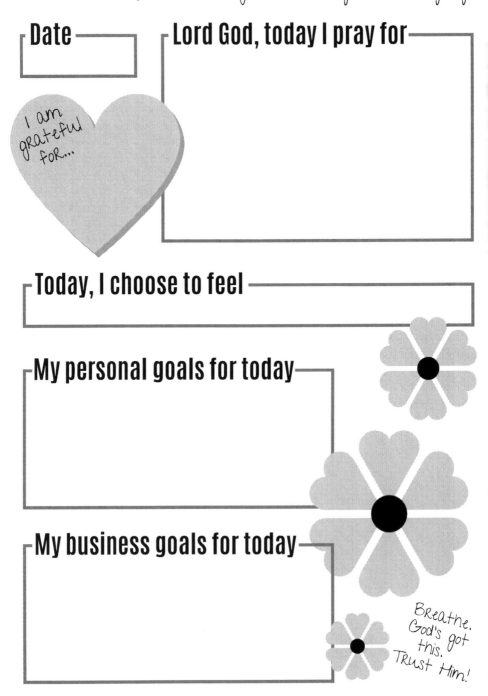

Date

Lord God, today I pray for

I am grateful for...

Today, I choose to feel

My personal goals for today

My business goals for today

Breathe. God's got this. Trust Him!

GOOD NIGHT EMPOWERED MAMA

am grateful for a life full of God's infinite blessings. My heart is open to what's next. I trust Him.

Lord God, thank you for

my favorite moment/memory from today was

Today, I felt

I achieved my personal goals | **Yes :: No**
I achieved my business goals | **Yes :: No**

How and why was I successful in my daily goals? What needs to change?

I trust in God's timing. Relax. Breathe. Rest.

I am strong. I am brave. I am loved. I am favored. I welcome God's provision and guidance today, and everyday.

Date

Lord God, today I pray for

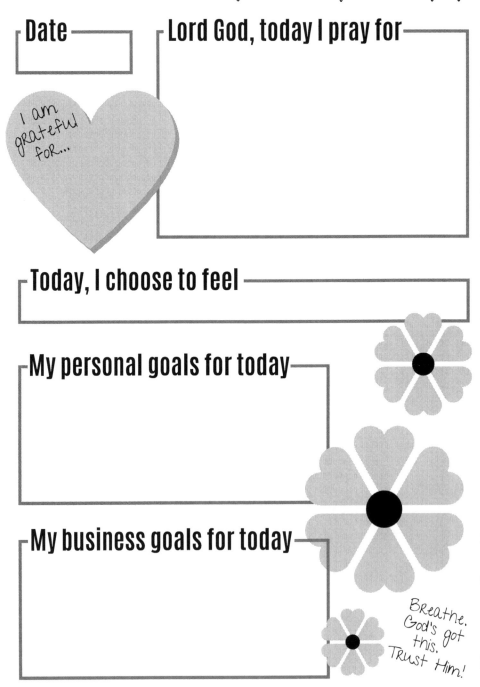

I am grateful for...

Today, I choose to feel

My personal goals for today

My business goals for today

Breathe. God's got this. Trust Him!

am grateful for a life full of God's infinite blessings. My heart is open to what's next. I trust Him.

Lord God, thank you for

my favorite moment/memory from today was

Today, I felt

I achieved my personal goals	**Yes :: No**
I achieved my business goals	**Yes :: No**

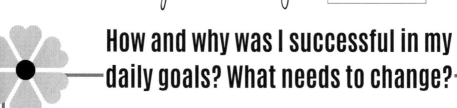

How and why was I successful in my daily goals? What needs to change?

I Trust in God's timing. Relax. Breathe. Rest.

I am strong. I am brave. I am loved. I am favored. I welcome God's provision and guidance today, and everyday.

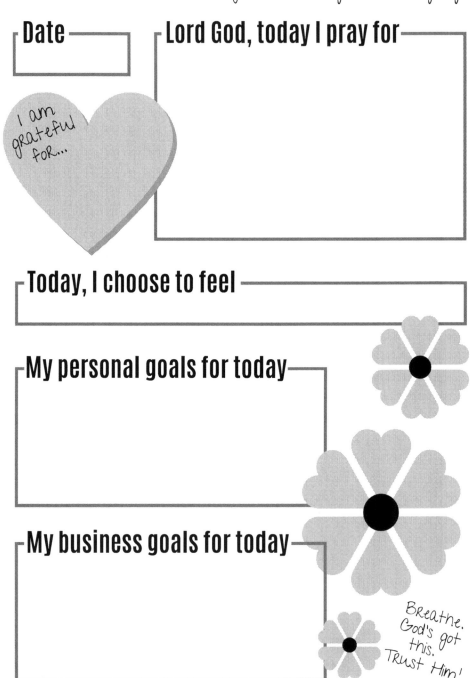

Date

Lord God, today I pray for

I am grateful for...

Today, I choose to feel

My personal goals for today

My business goals for today

Breathe. God's got this. Trust Him!

am grateful for a life full of God's infinite blessings. My heart is open to what's next. I trust Him.

Lord God, thank you for

my favorite moment/memory from today was

Today, I felt

I achieved my personal goals | Yes :: No

I achieved my business goals | Yes :: No

How and why was I successful in my daily goals? What needs to change?

Trust in God's timing. Relax. Breathe. Rest.

I am strong. I am brave. I am loved. I am favored. I welcome God's provision and guidance today, and everyday.

Date

Lord God, today I pray for

I am grateful for...

Today, I choose to feel

My personal goals for today

My business goals for today

Breathe. God's got this. Trust Him!

am grateful for a life full of God's infinite blessings. My heart is open to what's next. I trust Him.

Lord God, thank you for

my favorite moment/memory from today was

Today, I felt

I achieved my personal goals	Yes :: No
I achieved my business goals	Yes :: No

How and why was I successful in my daily goals? What needs to change?

I Trust in God's timing. Relax. Breathe. Rest.

I am strong. I am brave. I am loved. I am favored. I welcome God's provision and guidance today, and everyday.

Date

Lord God, today I pray for

I am grateful for...

Today, I choose to feel

My personal goals for today

My business goals for today

Breathe. God's got this. Trust Him!

am grateful for a life full of God's infinite blessings. My heart is open to what's Next. I trust Him.

Lord God, thank you for

my favorite moment/memory from today was

Today, I felt

I achieved my personal goals | Yes :: No
I achieved my business goals | Yes :: No

How and why was I successful in my daily goals? What needs to change?

Trust in God's timing. Relax. Breathe. Rest.

I am strong. I am brave. I am loved. I am favored. I welcome God's provision and guidance today, and everyday.

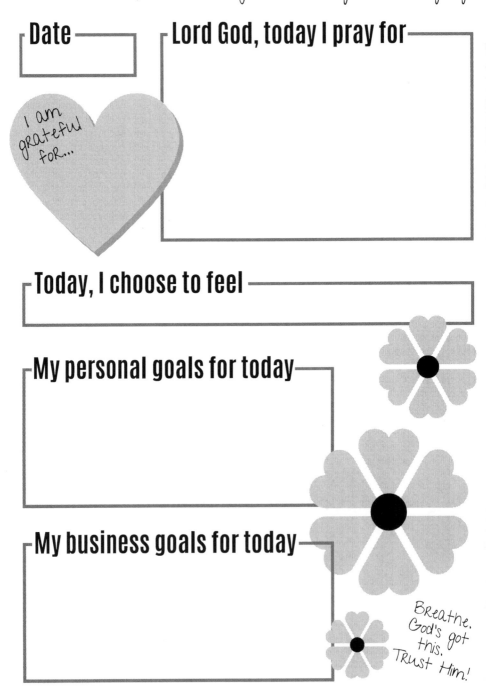

Date

Lord God, today I pray for

I am grateful for...

Today, I choose to feel

My personal goals for today

My business goals for today

Breathe. God's got this. Trust Him!

am grateful for a life full of God's infinite blessings. My heart is open to what's next. I trust Him.

Lord God, thank you for

my favorite moment/memory from today was

Today, I felt

I achieved my personal goals | Yes :: No

I achieved my business goals | Yes :: No

How and why was I successful in my daily goals? What needs to change?

I Trust in God's timing. Relax. Breathe. Rest.

I am strong. I am brave. I am loved. I am favored. I welcome God's provision and guidance today, and everyday.

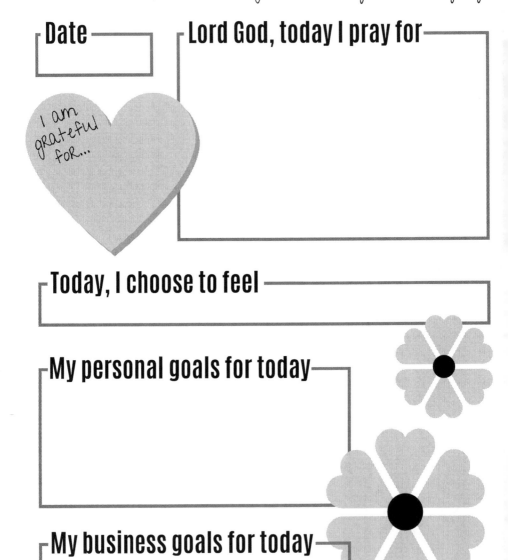

Date

Lord God, today I pray for

I am grateful for...

Today, I choose to feel

My personal goals for today

My business goals for today

Breathe. God's got this. Trust Him!

am grateful for a life full of God's infinite blessings. My heart is open to what's next. I trust Him.

Lord God, thank you for

my favorite moment/memory from today was

Today, I felt

I achieved my personal goals | Yes :: No
I achieved my business goals | Yes :: No

How and why was I successful in my daily goals? What needs to change?

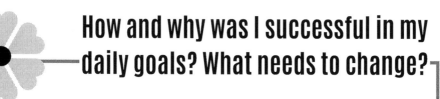

Trust in God's timing. Relax. Breathe. Rest.

I am strong. I am brave. I am loved. I am favored. I welcome God's provision and guidance today, and everyday.

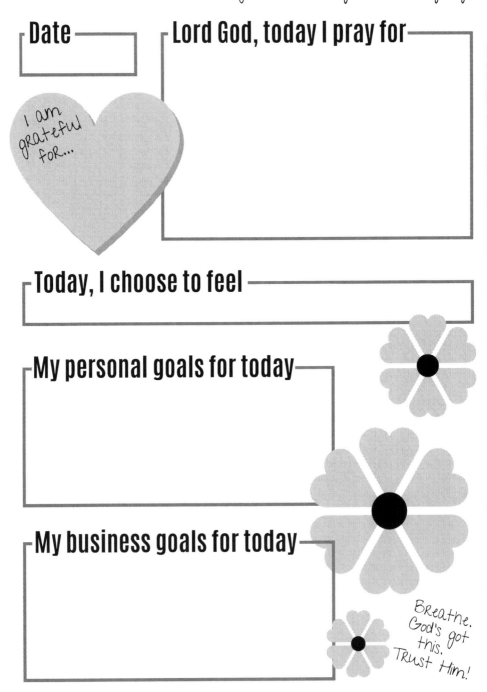

Date

Lord God, today I pray for

I am grateful for...

Today, I choose to feel

My personal goals for today

My business goals for today

Breathe. God's got this. Trust Him!

am grateful for a life full of God's infinite blessings. My heart is open to what's next. I trust Him.

Lord God, thank you for

my favorite moment/memory from today was

Today, I felt

I achieved my personal goals | Yes :: No
I achieved my business goals | Yes :: No

How and why was I successful in my daily goals? What needs to change?

Trust in God's timing. Relax. Breathe. Rest.

I am strong. I am brave. I am loved. I am favored. I welcome God's provision and guidance today, and everyday.

Date

I am grateful for...

Lord God, today I pray for

Today, I choose to feel

My personal goals for today

My business goals for today

Breathe. God's got this. Trust Him!

am grateful for a life full of God's infinite blessings. My heart is open to what's next. I trust Him.

Lord God, thank you for

my favorite moment/memory from today was

Today, I felt

I achieved my personal goals | Yes :: No
I achieved my business goals | Yes :: No

How and why was I successful in my daily goals? What needs to change?

Trust in God's timing. Relax. Breathe. Rest.

I am strong. I am brave. I am loved. I am favored. I welcome God's provision and guidance today, and everyday.

Date

Lord God, today I pray for

I am grateful for...

Today, I choose to feel

My personal goals for today

My business goals for today

Breathe. God's got this. Trust Him!

am grateful for a life full of God's infinite blessings. My heart is open to what's next. I trust Him.

Lord God, thank you for

my favorite moment/memory from today was

Today, I felt

I achieved my personal goals | Yes :: No
I achieved my business goals | Yes :: No

How and why was I successful in my daily goals? What needs to change?

I Trust in God's timing. Relax. Breathe. Rest.

I am strong. I am brave. I am loved. I am favored. I welcome God's provision and guidance today, and everyday.

Date

Lord God, today I pray for

I am grateful for...

Today, I choose to feel

My personal goals for today

My business goals for today

Breathe. God's got this. Trust Him!

am grateful for a life full of God's infinite blessings. My heart is open to what's next. I trust Him.

Lord God, thank you for

my favorite moment/memory from today was

Today, I felt

I achieved my personal goals | Yes :: No
I achieved my business goals | Yes :: No

How and why was I successful in my daily goals? What needs to change?

Trust in God's timing. Relax. Breathe. Rest.

I am strong. I am brave. I am loved. I am favored. I welcome God's provision and guidance today, and everyday.

Date

Lord God, today I pray for

I am grateful for...

Today, I choose to feel

My personal goals for today

My business goals for today

Breathe. God's got this. Trust Him!

am grateful for a life full of God's infinite blessings. my heart is open to what's next. I trust Him.

Lord God, thank you for

my favorite moment/memory from today was

Today, I felt

I achieved my personal goals | **Yes :: No**
I achieved my business goals | **Yes :: No**

How and why was I successful in my daily goals? What needs to change?

I trust in God's timing. Relax. Breathe. Rest.

I am stRoNg. I am bRave. I am loved. I am favoRed. I welcome God's pRovision and guidance today, and eveRyday.

Date

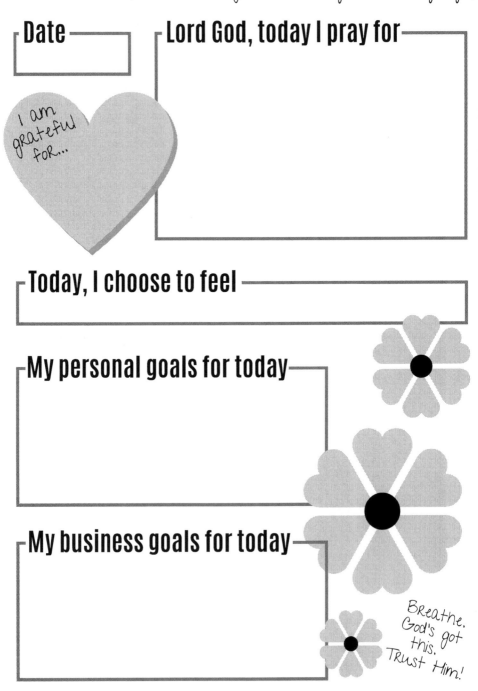

I am gRateful foR...

Lord God, today I pray for

Today, I choose to feel

My personal goals for today

My business goals for today

BReathe. God's got this. TRust Him!

am grateful for a life full of God's infinite blessings. My heart is open to what's next. I trust Him.

Lord God, thank you for

my favorite moment/memory from today was

Today, I felt

I achieved my personal goals | Yes :: No
I achieved my business goals | Yes :: No

How and why was I successful in my daily goals? What needs to change?

Trust in God's timing. Relax. Breathe. Rest.

I am stRoNG. I am bRave. I am loved. I am favoRed. I welcome God's pRovision and guidance today, and everyday.

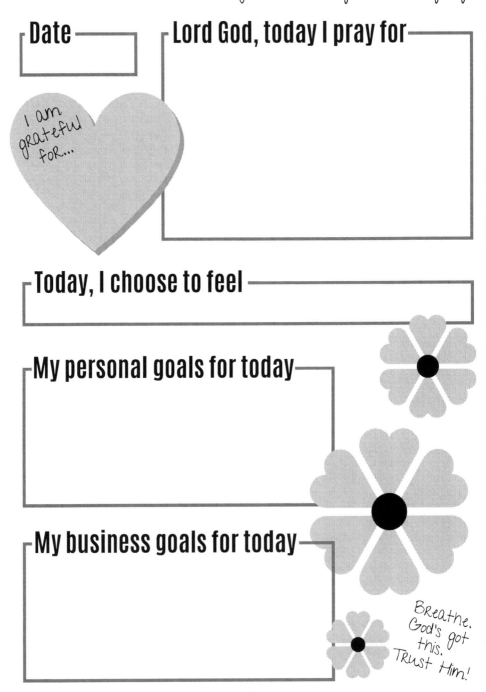

Date

Lord God, today I pray for

I am gRateful foR...

Today, I choose to feel

My personal goals for today

My business goals for today

BReathe. God's got this. TRust Him!

am grateful for a life full of God's infinite blessings. My
heart is open to what's next. I trust Him.

Lord God, thank you for

my favorite moment/memory from today was

Today, I felt

I achieved my personal goals | Yes :: No
I achieved my business goals | Yes :: No

How and why was I successful in my daily goals? What needs to change?

Trust in God's timing. Relax. Breathe. Rest.

I am strong. I am brave. I am loved. I am favored. I welcome God's provision and guidance today, and everyday.

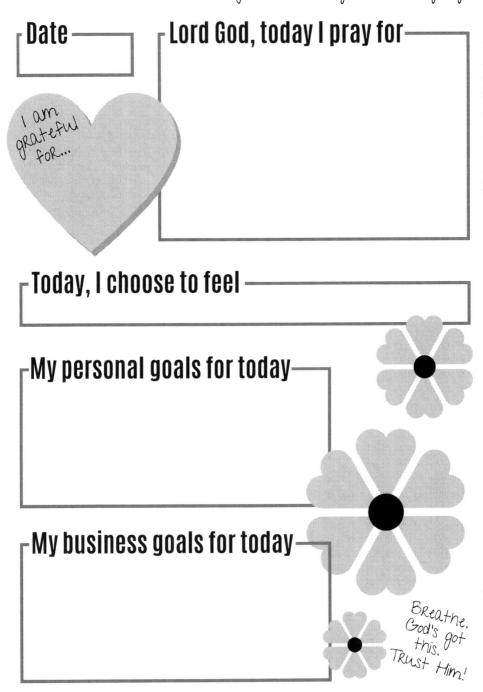

Date

Lord God, today I pray for

I am grateful for...

Today, I choose to feel

My personal goals for today

My business goals for today

Breathe. God's got this. Trust Him!

I am grateful for a life full of God's infinite blessings. My heart is open to what's next. I trust Him.

Lord God, thank you for

my favorite moment/memory from today was

Today, I felt

I achieved my personal goals | Yes :: No
I achieved my business goals | Yes :: No

How and why was I successful in my daily goals? What needs to change?

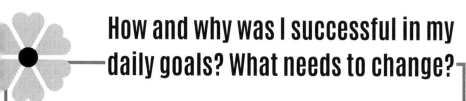

I Trust in God's timing. Relax. Breathe. Rest.

I am strong. I am brave. I am loved. I am favored. I welcome God's provision and guidance today, and everyday.

Date

Lord God, today I pray for

I am grateful for...

Today, I choose to feel

My personal goals for today

My business goals for today

Breathe. God's got this. Trust Him!

am grateful for a life full of God's infinite blessings. My heart is open to what's next. I trust Him.

Lord God, thank you for

my favorite moment/memory from today was

-Today, I felt-

I achieved my personal goals | Yes :: No
I achieved my business goals | Yes :: No

How and why was I successful in my daily goals? What needs to change?

Trust in God's timing. Relax. Breathe. Rest.

I am strong. I am brave. I am loved. I am favored. I welcome God's provision and guidance today, and everyday.

Date

Lord God, today I pray for

I am grateful for...

Today, I choose to feel

My personal goals for today

My business goals for today

Breathe. God's got this. Trust Him!

am grateful for a life full of God's infinite blessings. My heart is open to what's next. I trust Him.

Lord God, thank you for

my favorite moment/memory from today was

Today, I felt

I achieved my personal goals | Yes :: No
I achieved my business goals | Yes :: No

How and why was I successful in my daily goals? What needs to change?

I trust in God's timing. Relax. Breathe. Rest.

I am strong. I am brave. I am loved. I am favored. I welcome God's provision and guidance today, and everyday.

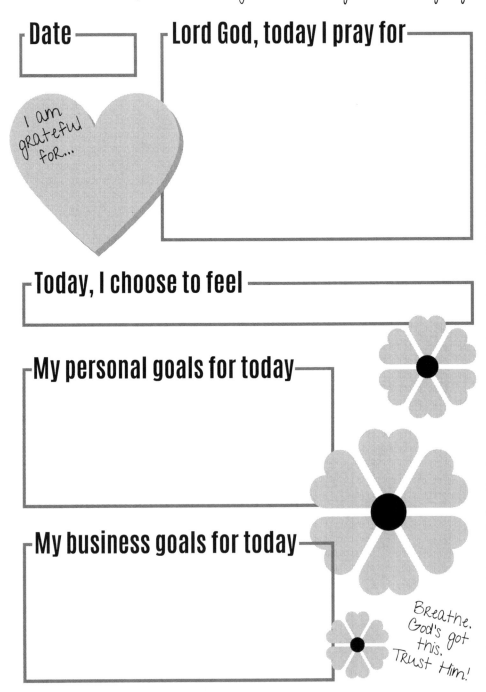

Date

Lord God, today I pray for

I am grateful for...

Today, I choose to feel

My personal goals for today

My business goals for today

Breathe. God's got this. Trust Him!

I am grateful for a life full of God's infinite blessings. My heart is open to what's next. I trust Him.

Lord God, thank you for

my favorite moment/memory from today was

Today, I felt

I achieved my personal goals | Yes :: No
I achieved my business goals | Yes :: No

How and why was I successful in my daily goals? What needs to change?

Trust in God's timing. Relax. Breathe. Rest.

I am strong. I am brave. I am loved. I am favored. I welcome God's provision and guidance today, and everyday.

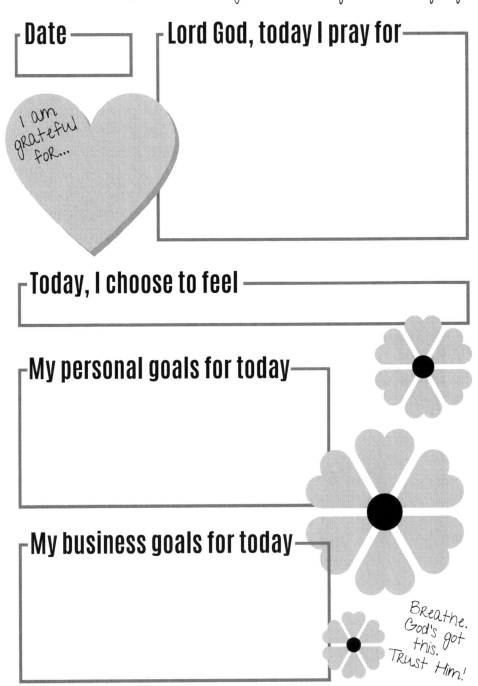

Date

Lord God, today I pray for

I am grateful for...

Today, I choose to feel

My personal goals for today

My business goals for today

Breathe. God's got this. Trust Him!

am grateful for a life full of God's infinite blessings. My heart is open to what's next. I trust Him.

Lord God, thank you for

my favorite moment/memory from today was

Today, I felt

I achieved my personal goals | Yes :: No

I achieved my business goals | Yes :: No

How and why was I successful in my daily goals? What needs to change?

Trust in God's timing. Relax. Breathe. Rest.

I am stRoNg. I am bRave. I am loved. I am favoRed. I welcome God's pRovision and guidance today, and everyday.

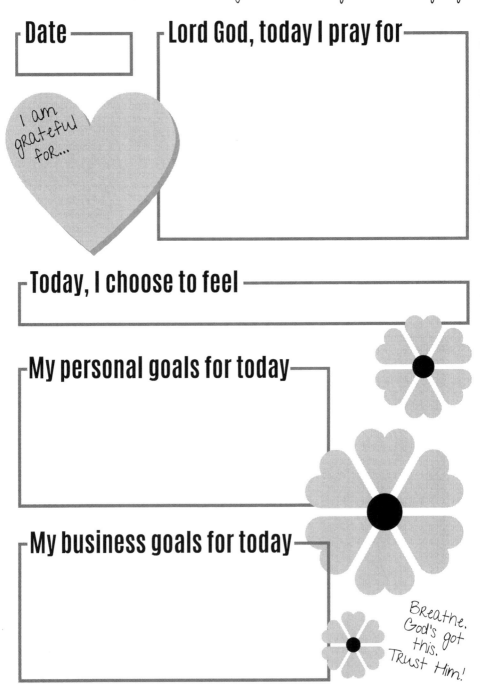

Date

Lord God, today I pray for

I am gRateful foR...

Today, I choose to feel

My personal goals for today

My business goals for today

BReathe. God's got this. TRust Him!

am grateful for a life full of God's infinite blessings. My heart is open to what's next. I trust Him.

Lord God, thank you for

my favorite moment/memory from today was

Today, I felt

I achieved my personal goals	Yes :: No
I achieved my business goals	Yes :: No

How and why was I successful in my daily goals? What needs to change?

Trust in God's timing. Relax. Breathe. Rest.

I am strong. I am brave. I am loved. I am favored. I welcome God's provision and guidance today, and everyday.

Date

Lord God, today I pray for

I am grateful for...

Today, I choose to feel

My personal goals for today

My business goals for today

Breathe. God's got this. Trust Him!

I am grateful for a life full of God's infinite blessings. My heart is open to what's next. I trust Him.

Lord God, thank you for

My favorite moment/memory from today was

Today, I felt

I achieved my personal goals	Yes :: No
I achieved my business goals	Yes :: No

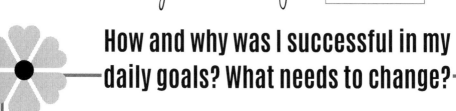

How and why was I successful in my daily goals? What needs to change?

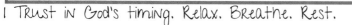

I trust in God's timing. Relax. Breathe. Rest.

I am strong. I am brave. I am loved. I am favored. I welcome God's provision and guidance today, and everyday.

Date

Lord God, today I pray for

I am grateful for...

Today, I choose to feel

My personal goals for today

My business goals for today

Breathe. God's got this. Trust Him!

am grateful for a life full of God's infinite blessings. My heart is open to what's next. I trust Him.

Lord God, thank you for

my favorite moment/memory from today was

Today, I felt

I achieved my personal goals | Yes :: No
I achieved my business goals | Yes :: No

How and why was I successful in my daily goals? What needs to change?

Trust in God's timing. Relax. Breathe. Rest.

I am strong. I am brave. I am loved. I am favored. I welcome God's provision and guidance today, and everyday.

Date

Lord God, today I pray for

I am grateful for...

Today, I choose to feel

My personal goals for today

My business goals for today

Breathe. God's got this. Trust Him!

am grateful for a life full of God's infinite blessings. My heart is open to what's next. I trust Him.

Lord God, thank you for

my favorite moment/memory from today was

Today, I felt

I achieved my personal goals | Yes :: No
I achieved my business goals | Yes :: No

How and why was I successful in my daily goals? What needs to change?

Trust in God's timing. Relax. Breathe. Rest.

I am strong. I am brave. I am loved. I am favored. I welcome God's provision and guidance today, and everyday.

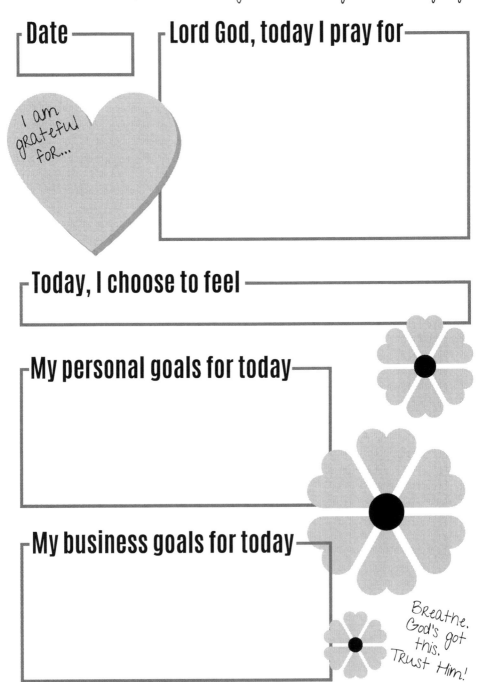

Date

Lord God, today I pray for

I am grateful for...

Today, I choose to feel

My personal goals for today

My business goals for today

Breathe. God's got this. Trust Him!

am grateful for a life full of God's infinite blessings. My heart is open to what's next. I trust Him.

Lord God, thank you for

my favorite moment/memory from today was

Today, I felt

I achieved my personal goals	Yes :: No
I achieved my business goals	Yes :: No

How and why was I successful in my daily goals? What needs to change?

Trust in God's timing. Relax. Breathe. Rest.

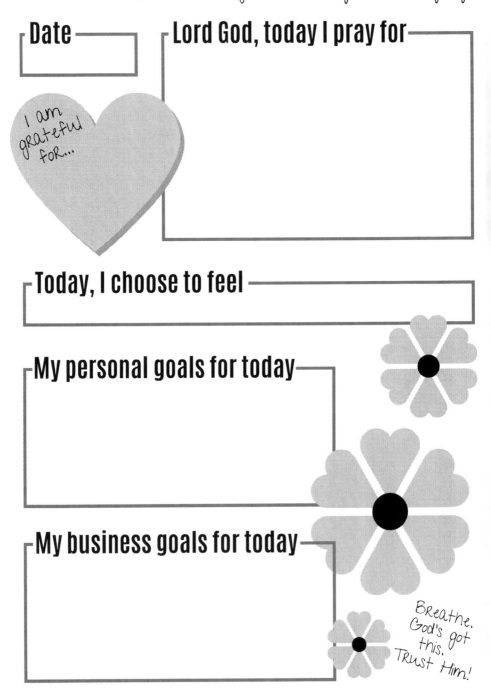

I am strong. I am brave. I am loved. I am favored. I welcome God's provision and guidance today, and everyday.

Date

Lord God, today I pray for

I am grateful for...

Today, I choose to feel

My personal goals for today

My business goals for today

Breathe. God's got this. Trust Him!

I am grateful for a life full of God's infinite blessings. My heart is open to what's next. I trust Him.

Lord God, thank you for

my favorite moment/memory from today was

Today, I felt

I achieved my personal goals | Yes :: No
I achieved my business goals | Yes :: No

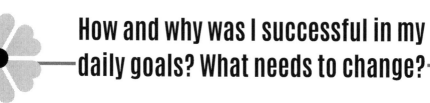

How and why was I successful in my daily goals? What needs to change?

Trust in God's timing. Relax. Breathe. Rest.

I am strong. I am brave. I am loved. I am favored. I welcome God's provision and guidance today, and everyday.

Date

Lord God, today I pray for

I am grateful for...

Today, I choose to feel

My personal goals for today

My business goals for today

Breathe. God's got this. Trust Him!

am grateful for a life full of God's infinite blessings. My heart is open to what's next. I trust Him.

Lord God, thank you for

my favorite moment/memory from today was

Today, I felt

I achieved my personal goals | **Yes :: No**
I achieved my business goals | **Yes :: No**

How and why was I successful in my daily goals? What needs to change?

Trust in God's timing. Relax. Breathe. Rest.

I am strong. I am brave. I am loved. I am favored. I welcome God's provision and guidance today, and everyday.

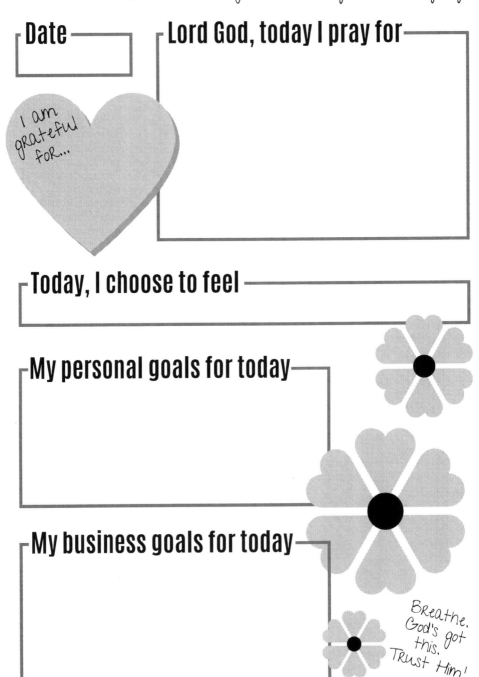

Date

Lord God, today I pray for

I am grateful for...

Today, I choose to feel

My personal goals for today

My business goals for today

Breathe. God's got this. Trust Him!

am grateful for a life full of God's infinite blessings. My heart is open to what's next. I trust Him.

Lord God, thank you for

my favorite moment/memory from today was

Today, I felt

I achieved my personal goals | Yes :: No
I achieved my business goals | Yes :: No

How and why was I successful in my daily goals? What needs to change?

Trust in God's timing. Relax. Breathe. Rest.

I am strong. I am brave. I am loved. I am favored. I welcome God's provision and guidance today, and everyday.

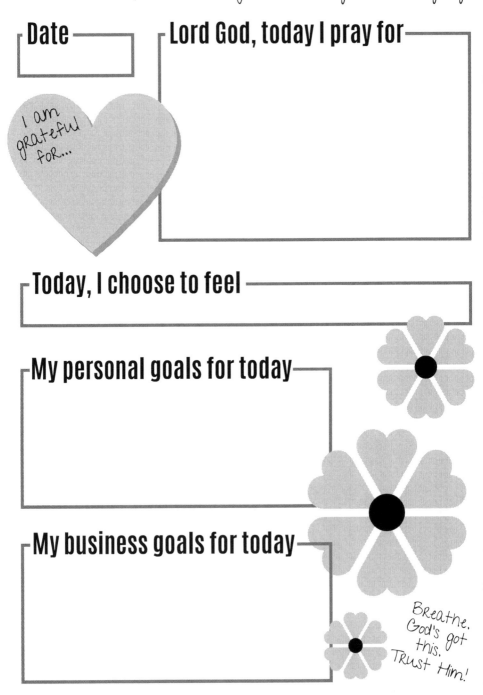

Date

Lord God, today I pray for

I am grateful for...

Today, I choose to feel

My personal goals for today

My business goals for today

Breathe. God's got this. Trust Him!

am grateful for a life full of God's infinite blessings. My heart is open to what's next. I trust Him.

Lord God, thank you for

my favorite moment/memory from today was

Today, I felt

I achieved my personal goals | Yes :: No

I achieved my business goals | Yes :: No

How and why was I successful in my daily goals? What needs to change?

I Trust in God's timing. Relax. Breathe. Rest.

I am strong. I am brave. I am loved. I am favored. I welcome God's provision and guidance today, and everyday.

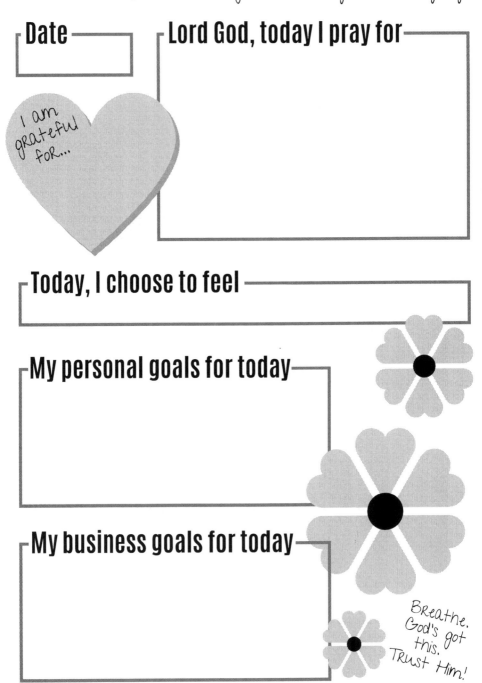

Date

Lord God, today I pray for

I am grateful for...

Today, I choose to feel

My personal goals for today

My business goals for today

Breathe. God's got this. Trust Him!

am grateful for a life full of God's infinite blessings. My heart is open to what's next. I trust Him.

Lord God, thank you for

my favorite moment/memory from today was

Today, I felt

I achieved my personal goals Yes :: No
I achieved my business goals Yes :: No

How and why was I successful in my daily goals? What needs to change?

Trust in God's timing. Relax. Breathe. Rest.

I am strong. I am brave. I am loved. I am favored. I welcome God's provision and guidance today, and everyday.

Date

Lord God, today I pray for

I am grateful for...

Today, I choose to feel

My personal goals for today

My business goals for today

Breathe. God's got this. Trust Him!

am grateful for a life full of God's infinite blessings. My
heart is open to what's next. I trust Him.

Lord God, thank you for

My favorite
moment/memory
from today was

Today, I felt

I achieved my personal goals | Yes :: No
I achieved my business goals | Yes :: No

How and why was I successful in my daily goals? What needs to change?

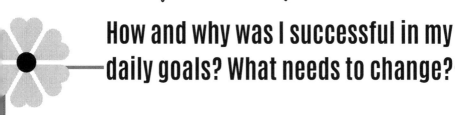

Trust in God's timing. Relax. Breathe. Rest.

I am strong. I am brave. I am loved. I am favored. I welcome God's provision and guidance today, and everyday.

Date

Lord God, today I pray for

I am grateful for...

Today, I choose to feel

My personal goals for today

My business goals for today

Breathe. God's got this. Trust Him!

I am grateful for a life full of God's infinite blessings. My heart is open to what's next. I trust Him.

Lord God, thank you for

my favorite moment/memory from today was

Today, I felt

I achieved my personal goals | Yes :: No
I achieved my business goals | Yes :: No

How and why was I successful in my daily goals? What needs to change?

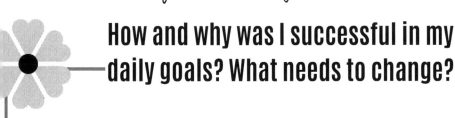

I trust in God's timing. Relax. Breathe. Rest.

I am strong. I am brave. I am loved. I am favored. I welcome God's provision and guidance today, and everyday.

Date

Lord God, today I pray for

I am grateful for...

Today, I choose to feel

My personal goals for today

My business goals for today

Breathe. God's got this. Trust Him!

am grateful for a life full of God's infinite blessings. My heart is open to what's next. I trust Him.

Lord God, thank you for

my favorite moment/memory from today was

Today, I felt

| I achieved my personal goals | Yes :: No |
| I achieved my business goals | Yes :: No |

How and why was I successful in my daily goals? What needs to change?

Trust in God's timing. Relax. Breathe. Rest.

I am strong. I am brave. I am loved. I am favored. I welcome God's provision and guidance today, and everyday.

Date

Lord God, today I pray for

I am grateful for...

Today, I choose to feel

My personal goals for today

My business goals for today

Breathe. God's got this. Trust Him!

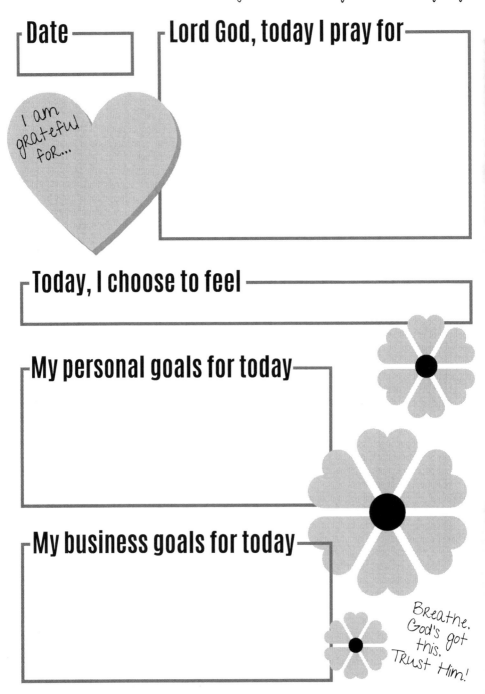

am grateful for a life full of God's infinite blessings. My heart is open to what's next. I trust Him.

Lord God, thank you for

my favorite moment/memory from today was

Today, I felt

I achieved my personal goals | Yes :: No
I achieved my business goals | Yes :: No

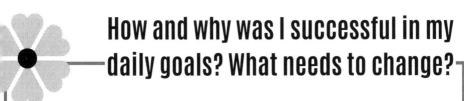

How and why was I successful in my daily goals? What needs to change?

I Trust in God's timing. Relax. Breathe. Rest.

I am stRoNG. I am bRave. I am loved. I am favoRed. I welcome God's pRovisioN and guidance today, and eveRyday.

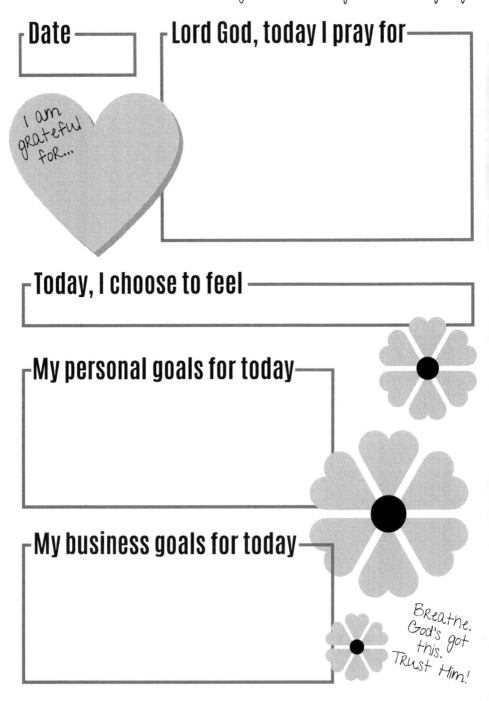

Date

Lord God, today I pray for

I am gRateful foR...

Today, I choose to feel

My personal goals for today

My business goals for today

BReathe. God's got this. TRust Him!

am grateful for a life full of God's infinite blessings. My heart is open to what's next. I trust Him.

Lord God, thank you for

my favorite moment/memory from today was

Today, I felt

I achieved my personal goals | Yes :: No

I achieved my business goals | Yes :: No

How and why was I successful in my daily goals? What needs to change?

I trust in God's timing. Relax. Breathe. Rest.

I am strong. I am brave. I am loved. I am favored. I welcome God's provision and guidance today, and everyday.

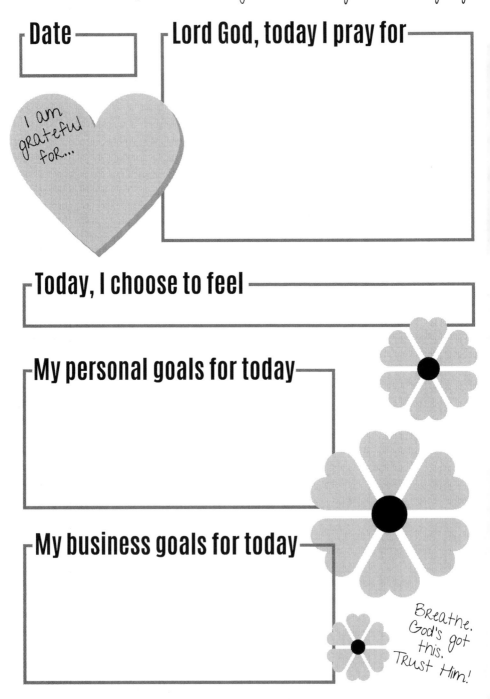

Date

I am grateful for...

Lord God, today I pray for

Today, I choose to feel

My personal goals for today

My business goals for today

Breathe. God's got this. Trust Him!

am grateful for a life full of God's infinite blessings. My heart is open to what's next. I trust Him.

Lord God, thank you for

my favorite moment/memory from today was

Today, I felt

I achieved my personal goals | Yes :: No
I achieved my business goals | Yes :: No

How and why was I successful in my daily goals? What needs to change?

Trust in God's timing. Relax. Breathe. Rest.

I am strong. I am brave. I am loved. I am favored. I welcome God's provision and guidance today, and everyday.

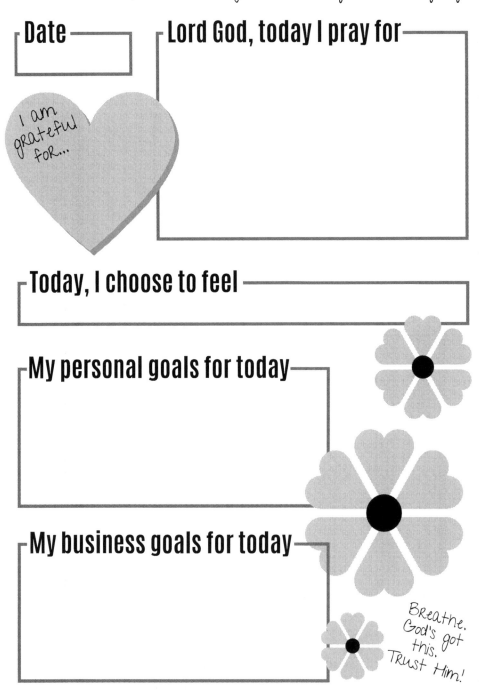

Date

Lord God, today I pray for

I am grateful for...

Today, I choose to feel

My personal goals for today

My business goals for today

Breathe. God's got this. Trust Him!

am grateful for a life full of God's infinite blessings. My heart is open to what's next. I trust Him.

Lord God, thank you for

my favorite moment/memory from today was

Today, I felt

I achieved my personal goals | Yes :: No
I achieved my business goals | Yes :: No

How and why was I successful in my daily goals? What needs to change?

Trust in God's timing. Relax. Breathe. Rest.

I am strong. I am brave. I am loved. I am favored. I welcome God's provision and guidance today, and everyday.

Date

Lord God, today I pray for

I am grateful for...

Today, I choose to feel

My personal goals for today

My business goals for today

Breathe. God's got this. Trust Him!

am grateful for a life full of God's infinite blessings. My heart is open to what's next. I trust Him.

Lord God, thank you for

my favorite moment/memory from today was

Today, I felt

I achieved my personal goals | Yes :: No
I achieved my business goals | Yes :: No

How and why was I successful in my daily goals? What needs to change?

I Trust in God's timing. Relax. Breathe. Rest.

I am strong. I am brave. I am loved. I am favored. I welcome God's provision and guidance today, and everyday.

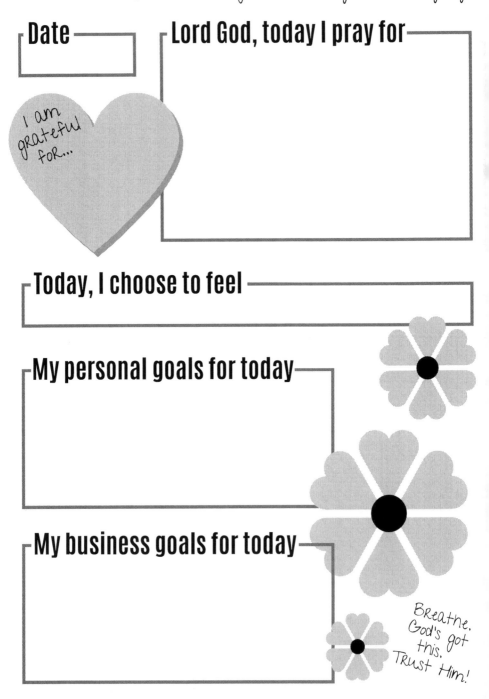

Date

Lord God, today I pray for

I am grateful for...

Today, I choose to feel

My personal goals for today

My business goals for today

Breathe. God's got this. Trust Him!

I am grateful for a life full of God's infinite blessings. My heart is open to what's next. I trust Him.

Lord God, thank you for

my favorite moment/memory from today was

Today, I felt

I achieved my personal goals | Yes :: No
I achieved my business goals | Yes :: No

How and why was I successful in my daily goals? What needs to change?

I trust in God's timing. Relax. Breathe. Rest.

I am stRong. I am bRave. I am loved. I am favoRed. I welcome God's pRovision and guidance today, and everyday.

Date

Lord God, today I pray for

I am gRateful foR...

Today, I choose to feel

My personal goals for today

My business goals for today

Breathe. God's got this. TRust Him!

I am grateful for a life full of God's infinite blessings. My heart is open to what's next. I trust Him.

Lord God, thank you for

my favorite moment/memory from today was

Today, I felt

I achieved my personal goals | Yes :: No
I achieved my business goals | Yes :: No

How and why was I successful in my daily goals? What needs to change?

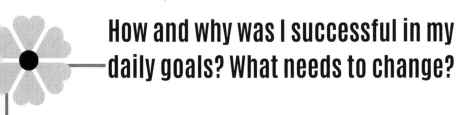

I Trust in God's timing. Relax. Breathe. Rest.

I am strong. I am brave. I am loved. I am favored. I welcome God's provision and guidance today, and everyday.

Date

Lord God, today I pray for

I am grateful for...

Today, I choose to feel

My personal goals for today

My business goals for today

Breathe. God's got this. Trust Him!

am grateful for a life full of God's infinite blessings. My heart is open to what's next. I trust Him.

Lord God, thank you for

my favorite moment/memory from today was

Today, I felt

I achieved my personal goals Yes :: No
I achieved my business goals Yes :: No

How and why was I successful in my daily goals? What needs to change?

Trust in God's timing. Relax. Breathe. Rest.

I am strong. I am brave. I am loved. I am favored. I welcome God's provision and guidance today, and everyday.

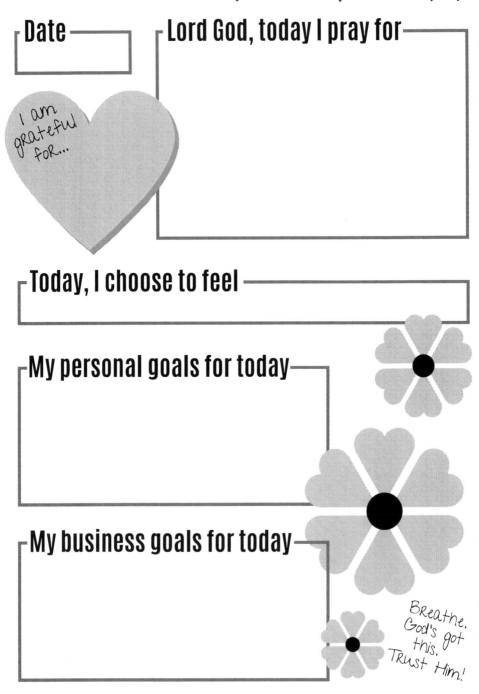

Date

Lord God, today I pray for

I am grateful for...

Today, I choose to feel

My personal goals for today

My business goals for today

Breathe. God's got this. Trust Him!

I am grateful for a life full of God's infinite blessings. My heart is open to what's next. I trust Him.

Lord God, thank you for

my favorite moment/memory from today was

Today, I felt

I achieved my personal goals | **Yes :: No**
I achieved my business goals | **Yes :: No**

How and why was I successful in my daily goals? What needs to change?

I trust in God's timing. Relax. Breathe. Rest.

I am strong. I am brave. I am loved. I am favored. I welcome God's provision and guidance today, and everyday.

Date

Lord God, today I pray for

I am grateful for...

Today, I choose to feel

My personal goals for today

My business goals for today

Breathe. God's got this. Trust Him!

I am grateful for a life full of God's infinite blessings. My heart is open to what's next. I trust Him.

Lord God, thank you for

my favorite moment/memory from today was

Today, I felt

I achieved my personal goals | Yes :: No
I achieved my business goals | Yes :: No

How and why was I successful in my daily goals? What needs to change?

I trust in God's timing. Relax. Breathe. Rest.

I am strong. I am brave. I am loved. I am favored. I welcome God's provision and guidance today, and everyday.

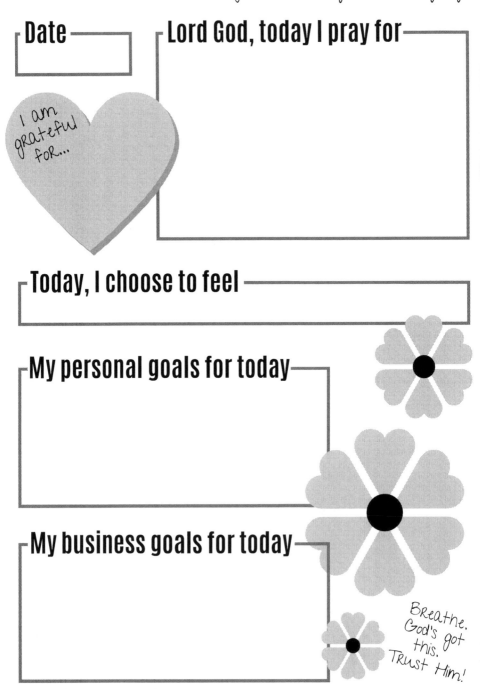

Date

Lord God, today I pray for

I am grateful for...

Today, I choose to feel

My personal goals for today

My business goals for today

Breathe. God's got this. Trust Him!

am grateful for a life full of God's infinite blessings. My heart is open to what's next. I trust Him.

Lord God, thank you for

my favorite moment/memory from today was

Today, I felt

I achieved my personal goals   Yes :: No
I achieved my business goals   Yes :: No

How and why was I successful in my daily goals? What needs to change?

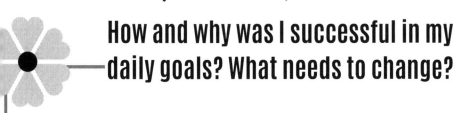

I trust in God's timing. Relax. Breathe. Rest.

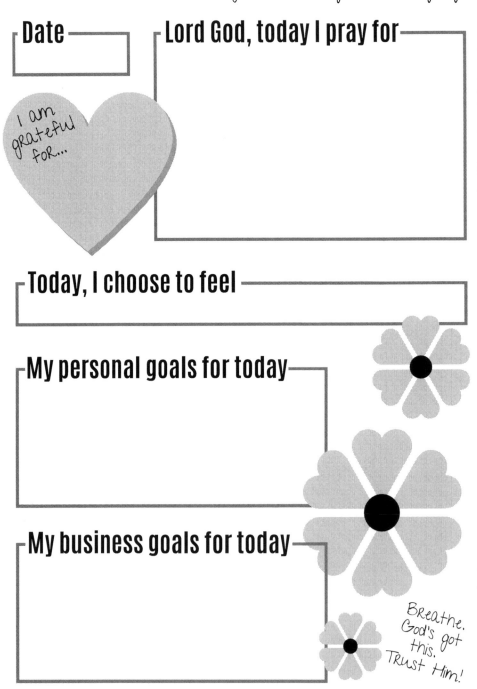

I am strong. I am brave. I am loved. I am favored. I welcome God's provision and guidance today, and everyday.

Date

Lord God, today I pray for

I am grateful for...

Today, I choose to feel

My personal goals for today

My business goals for today

Breathe. God's got this. Trust Him!

I am grateful for a life full of God's infinite blessings. My heart is open to what's next. I trust Him.

Lord God, thank you for

my favorite moment/memory from today was

Today, I felt

I achieved my personal goals | Yes :: No
I achieved my business goals | Yes :: No

How and why was I successful in my daily goals? What needs to change?

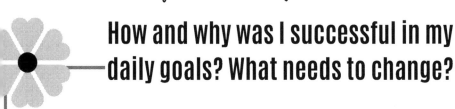

I trust in God's timing. Relax. Breathe. Rest.

I am strong. I am brave. I am loved. I am favored. I welcome God's provision and guidance today, and everyday.

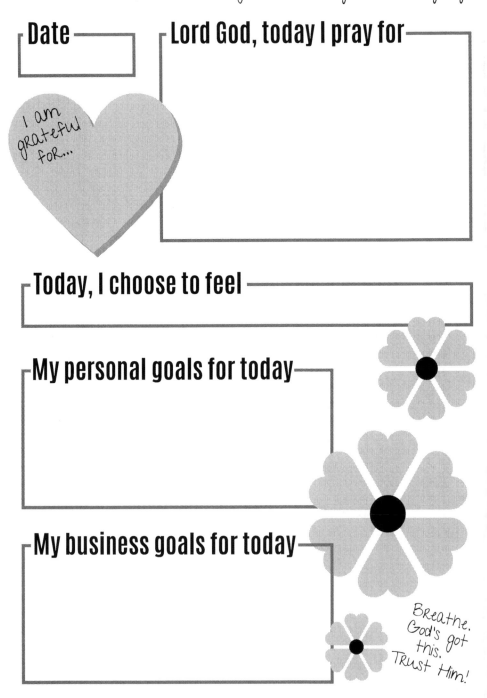

Date

Lord God, today I pray for

I am grateful for...

Today, I choose to feel

My personal goals for today

My business goals for today

Breathe. God's got this. Trust Him!

am grateful for a life full of God's infinite blessings. My heart is open to what's next. I trust Him.

Lord God, thank you for

my favorite moment/memory from today was

Today, I felt

I achieved my personal goals | Yes :: No
I achieved my business goals | Yes :: No

How and why was I successful in my daily goals? What needs to change?

Trust in God's timing. Relax. Breathe. Rest.

GOOD MORNING COURAGEOUS MAMA

I am strong. I am brave. I am loved. I am favored. I welcome God's provision and guidance today, and everyday.

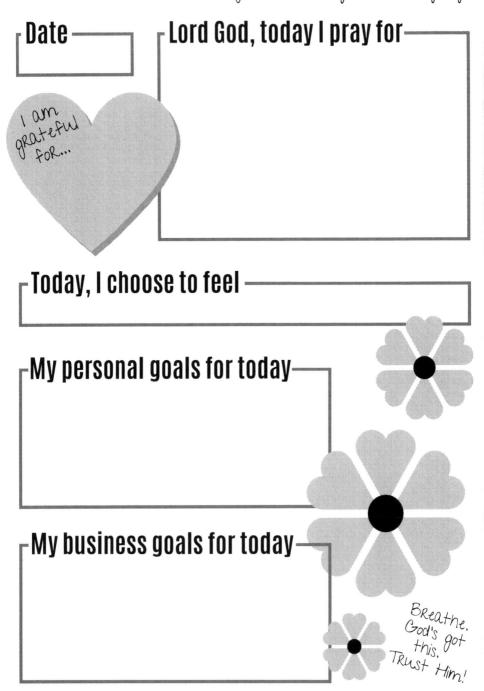

Date

Lord God, today I pray for

I am grateful for...

Today, I choose to feel

My personal goals for today

My business goals for today

Breathe. God's got this. Trust Him!

am grateful for a life full of God's infinite blessings. My heart is open to what's next. I trust Him.

Lord God, thank you for

my favorite moment/memory from today was

Today, I felt

I achieved my personal goals | Yes :: No
I achieved my business goals | Yes :: No

How and why was I successful in my daily goals? What needs to change?

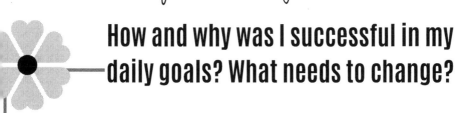

I Trust in God's timing. Relax. Breathe. Rest.

I am strong. I am brave. I am loved. I am favored. I welcome God's provision and guidance today, and everyday.

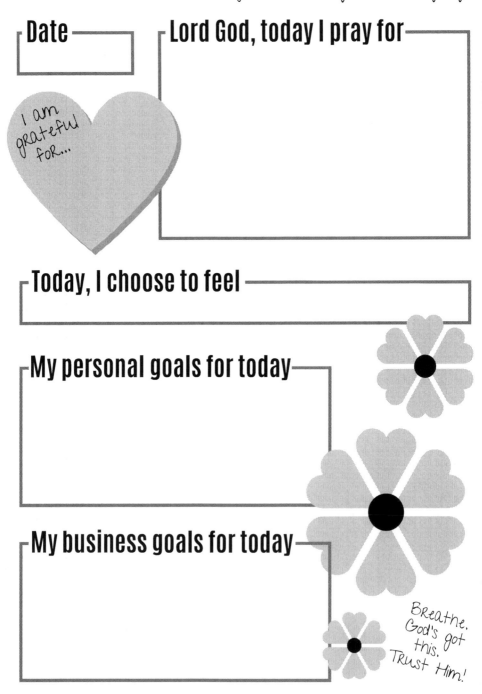

Date

Lord God, today I pray for

I am grateful for...

Today, I choose to feel

My personal goals for today

My business goals for today

Breathe. God's got this. Trust Him!

am grateful for a life full of God's infinite blessings. My heart is open to what's next. I trust Him.

Lord God, thank you for

my favorite moment/memory from today was

Today, I felt

I achieved my personal goals | Yes :: No
I achieved my business goals | Yes :: No

How and why was I successful in my daily goals? What needs to change?

Trust in God's timing. Relax. Breathe. Rest.

I am strong. I am brave. I am loved. I am favored. I welcome God's provision and guidance today, and everyday.

Date

Lord God, today I pray for

I am grateful for...

Today, I choose to feel

My personal goals for today

My business goals for today

Breathe. God's got this. Trust Him!

I am grateful for a life full of God's infinite blessings. My heart is open to what's next. I trust Him.

Lord God, thank you for

my favorite moment/memory from today was

Today, I felt

I achieved my personal goals | Yes :: No
I achieved my business goals | Yes :: No

How and why was I successful in my daily goals? What needs to change?

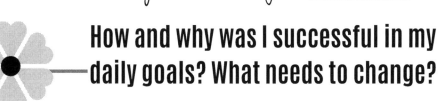

I trust in God's timing. Relax. Breathe. Rest.

I am strong. I am brave. I am loved. I am favored. I welcome God's provision and guidance today, and everyday.

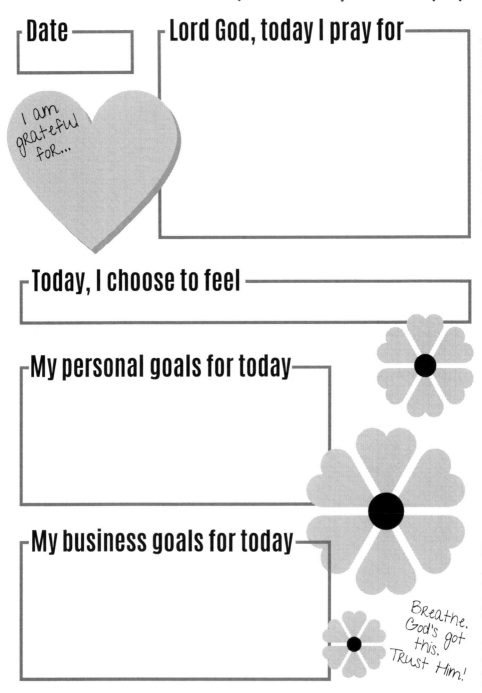

Date

Lord God, today I pray for

I am grateful for...

Today, I choose to feel

My personal goals for today

My business goals for today

Breathe. God's got this. Trust Him!

I am grateful for a life full of God's infinite blessings. My heart is open to what's next. I trust Him.

Lord God, thank you for

my favorite moment/memory from today was

Today, I felt

I achieved my personal goals | Yes :: No
I achieved my business goals | Yes :: No

How and why was I successful in my daily goals? What needs to change?

I trust in God's timing. Relax. Breathe. Rest.

I am strong. I am brave. I am loved. I am favored. I welcome God's provision and guidance today, and everyday.

Date

Lord God, today I pray for

I am grateful for...

Today, I choose to feel

My personal goals for today

My business goals for today

Breathe. God's got this. Trust Him!

am grateful for a life full of God's infinite blessings. My heart is open to what's next. I trust Him.

Lord God, thank you for

my favorite moment/memory from today was

Today, I felt

I achieved my personal goals | Yes :: No
I achieved my business goals | Yes :: No

How and why was I successful in my daily goals? What needs to change?

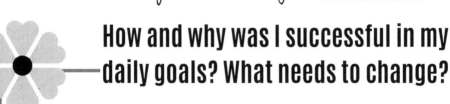

I trust in God's timing. Relax. Breathe. Rest.

I am strong. I am brave. I am loved. I am favored. I welcome God's provision and guidance today, and everyday.

Date

Lord God, today I pray for

I am grateful for...

Today, I choose to feel

My personal goals for today

My business goals for today

Breathe. God's got this. Trust Him!

am grateful for a life full of God's infinite blessings. My heart is open to what's next. I trust Him.

Lord God, thank you for

my favorite moment/memory from today was

Today, I felt

I achieved my personal goals | Yes :: No
I achieved my business goals | Yes :: No

How and why was I successful in my daily goals? What needs to change?

Trust in God's timing. Relax. Breathe. Rest.

I am strong. I am brave. I am loved. I am favored. I welcome God's provision and guidance today, and everyday.

Date

Lord God, today I pray for

I am grateful for...

Today, I choose to feel

My personal goals for today

My business goals for today

Breathe. God's got this. Trust Him!

I am grateful for a life full of God's infinite blessings. My heart is open to what's next. I trust Him.

Lord God, thank you for

my favorite moment/memory from today was

Today, I felt

I achieved my personal goals | Yes :: No
I achieved my business goals | Yes :: No

How and why was I successful in my daily goals? What needs to change?

I trust in God's timing. Relax. Breathe. Rest.

I am strong. I am brave. I am loved. I am favored. I welcome God's provision and guidance today, and everyday.

Date

Lord God, today I pray for

I am grateful for...

Today, I choose to feel

My personal goals for today

My business goals for today

Breathe. God's got this. Trust Him!

am grateful for a life full of God's infinite blessings. My heart is open to what's next. I trust Him.

Lord God, thank you for

my favorite moment/memory from today was

Today, I felt

I achieved my personal goals | Yes :: No
I achieved my business goals | Yes :: No

How and why was I successful in my daily goals? What needs to change?

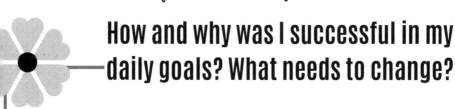

Trust in God's timing. Relax. Breathe. Rest.

I am strong. I am brave. I am loved. I am favored. I welcome God's provision and guidance today, and everyday.

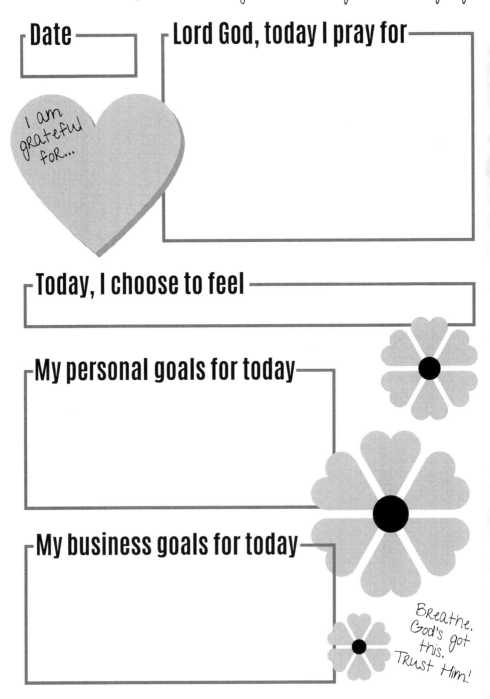

Date

Lord God, today I pray for

I am grateful for...

Today, I choose to feel

My personal goals for today

My business goals for today

Breathe. God's got this. Trust Him!

am grateful for a life full of God's infinite blessings. My heart is open to what's next. I trust Him.

Lord God, thank you for

my favorite moment/memory from today was

Today, I felt

I achieved my personal goals | Yes :: No
I achieved my business goals | Yes :: No

How and why was I successful in my daily goals? What needs to change?

Trust in God's timing. Relax. Breathe. Rest.

I am strong. I am brave. I am loved. I am favored. I welcome God's provision and guidance today, and everyday.

Date

Lord God, today I pray for

I am grateful for...

Today, I choose to feel

My personal goals for today

My business goals for today

Breathe. God's got this. Trust Him!

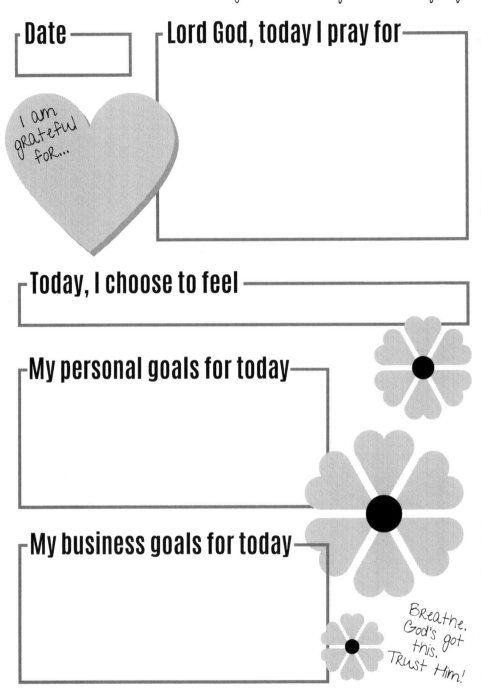

GOOD NIGHT EMPOWERED MAMA

I am grateful for a life full of God's infinite blessings. My heart is open to what's next. I trust Him.

Lord God, thank you for

my favorite moment/memory from today was

Today, I felt

I achieved my personal goals **Yes :: No**
I achieved my business goals **Yes :: No**

How and why was I successful in my daily goals? What needs to change?

Trust in God's timing. Relax. Breathe. Rest.

I am strong. I am brave. I am loved. I am favored. I welcome God's provision and guidance today, and everyday.

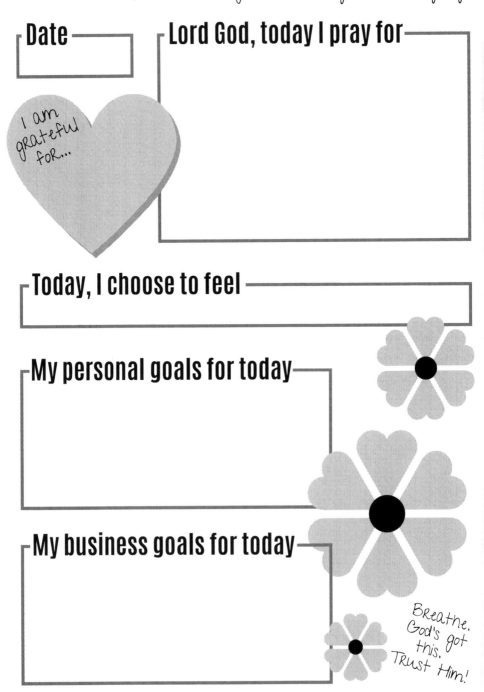

Date

Lord God, today I pray for

I am grateful for...

Today, I choose to feel

My personal goals for today

My business goals for today

Breathe. God's got this. Trust Him!

am grateful for a life full of God's infinite blessings. my heart is open to what's next. I trust Him.

Lord God, thank you for

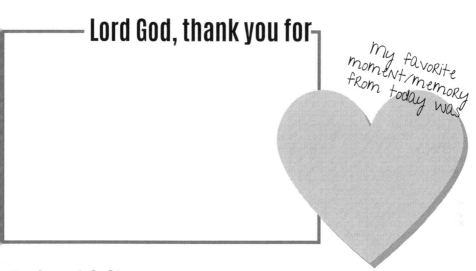

my favorite moment/memory from today was

Today, I felt

I achieved my personal goals | Yes :: No
I achieved my business goals | Yes :: No

How and why was I successful in my daily goals? What needs to change?

I Trust in God's timing. Relax. Breathe. Rest.

I am strong. I am brave. I am loved. I am favored. I welcome God's provision and guidance today, and everyday.

Date

Lord God, today I pray for

I am grateful for...

Today, I choose to feel

My personal goals for today

My business goals for today

Breathe. God's got this. Trust Him!

I am grateful for a life full of God's infinite blessings. My heart is open to what's next. I trust Him.

Lord God, thank you for

my favorite moment/memory from today was

Today, I felt

I achieved my personal goals | **Yes :: No**
I achieved my business goals | **Yes :: No**

How and why was I successful in my daily goals? What needs to change?

I Trust in God's timing. Relax. Breathe. Rest.

I am strong. I am brave. I am loved. I am favored. I welcome God's provision and guidance today, and everyday.

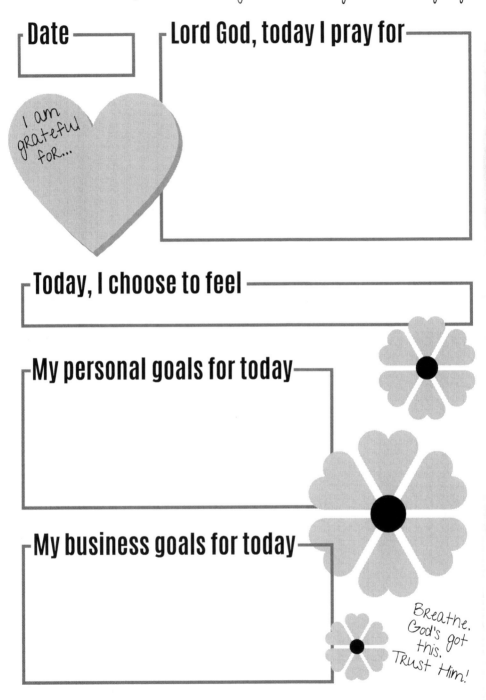

Date

Lord God, today I pray for

I am grateful for...

Today, I choose to feel

My personal goals for today

My business goals for today

Breathe. God's got this. Trust Him!

am grateful for a life full of God's infinite blessings. My
heart is open to what's next. I trust Him.

Lord God, thank you for

my favorite
moment/memory
from today was

Today, I felt

I achieved my personal goals | Yes :: No
I achieved my business goals | Yes :: No

How and why was I successful in my daily goals? What needs to change?

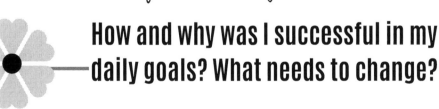

I Trust in God's timing. Relax. Breathe. Rest.

I am strong. I am brave. I am loved. I am favored. I welcome God's provision and guidance today, and everyday.

Date

Lord God, today I pray for

I am grateful for...

Today, I choose to feel

My personal goals for today

My business goals for today

Breathe. God's got this. Trust Him!

I am grateful for a life full of God's infinite blessings. My heart is open to what's next. I trust Him.

Lord God, thank you for

my favorite moment/memory from today was

Today, I felt

I achieved my personal goals | Yes :: No

I achieved my business goals | Yes :: No

How and why was I successful in my daily goals? What needs to change?

I trust in God's timing. Relax. Breathe. Rest.

I am strong. I am brave. I am loved. I am favored. I welcome God's provision and guidance today, and everyday.

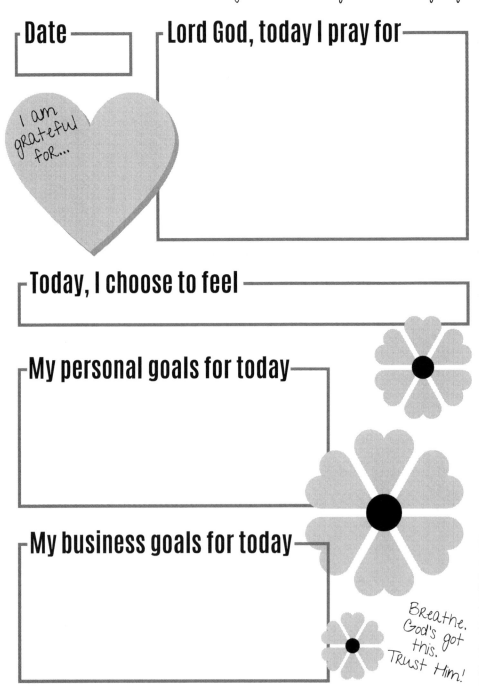

Date

Lord God, today I pray for

I am grateful for...

Today, I choose to feel

My personal goals for today

My business goals for today

Breathe. God's got this. Trust Him!

am grateful for a life full of God's infinite blessings. My heart is open to what's next. I trust Him.

Lord God, thank you for

my favorite moment/memory from today was

Today, I felt

I achieved my personal goals | Yes :: No

I achieved my business goals | Yes :: No

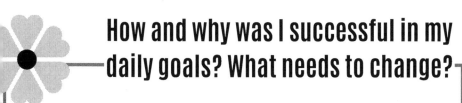

How and why was I successful in my daily goals? What needs to change?

Trust in God's timing. Relax. Breathe. Rest.

I am strong. I am brave. I am loved. I am favored. I welcome God's provision and guidance today, and everyday.

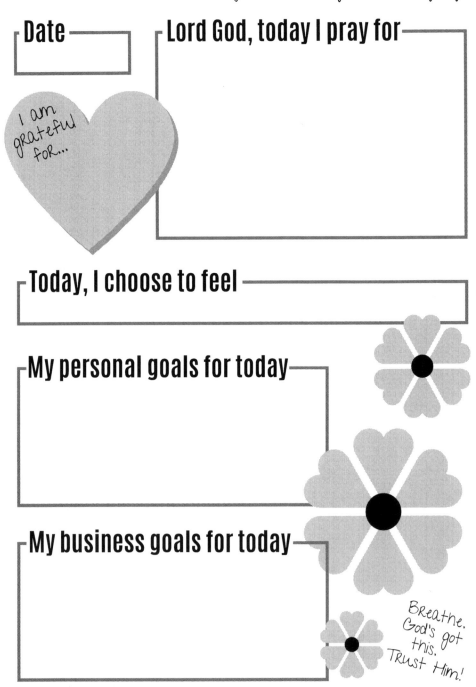

Date

Lord God, today I pray for

I am grateful for...

Today, I choose to feel

My personal goals for today

My business goals for today

Breathe. God's got this. Trust Him!

am grateful for a life full of God's infinite blessings. My heart is open to what's next. I trust Him.

Lord God, thank you for

my favorite moment/memory from today was

Today, I felt

I achieved my personal goals | Yes :: No

I achieved my business goals | Yes :: No

How and why was I successful in my daily goals? What needs to change?

I Trust in God's timing. Relax. Breathe. Rest.

I am strong. I am brave. I am loved. I am favored. I welcome God's provision and guidance today, and everyday.

Date

Lord God, today I pray for

I am grateful for...

Today, I choose to feel

My personal goals for today

My business goals for today

Breathe. God's got this. Trust Him!

am grateful for a life full of God's infinite blessings. My heart is open to what's next. I trust Him.

Lord God, thank you for

my favorite moment/memory from today was

Today, I felt

I achieved my personal goals | Yes :: No
I achieved my business goals | Yes :: No

How and why was I successful in my daily goals? What needs to change?

Trust in God's timing. Relax. Breathe. Rest.

I am strong. I am brave. I am loved. I am favored. I welcome God's provision and guidance today, and everyday.

Date

Lord God, today I pray for

I am grateful for...

Today, I choose to feel

My personal goals for today

My business goals for today

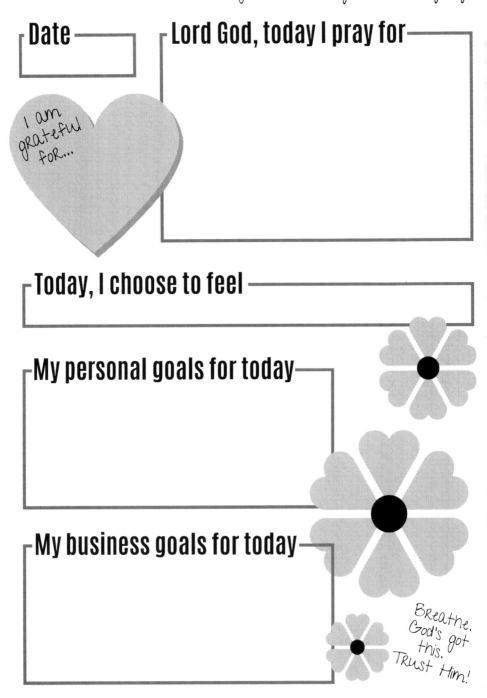

Breathe. God's got this. Trust Him!

am grateful for a life full of God's infinite blessings. My heart is open to what's next. I trust Him.

Lord God, thank you for

my favorite moment/memory from today was

Today, I felt

I achieved my personal goals | Yes :: No
I achieved my business goals | Yes :: No

How and why was I successful in my daily goals? What needs to change?

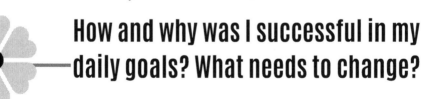

I trust in God's timing. Relax. Breathe. Rest.

I am strong. I am brave. I am loved. I am favored. I welcome God's provision and guidance today, and everyday.

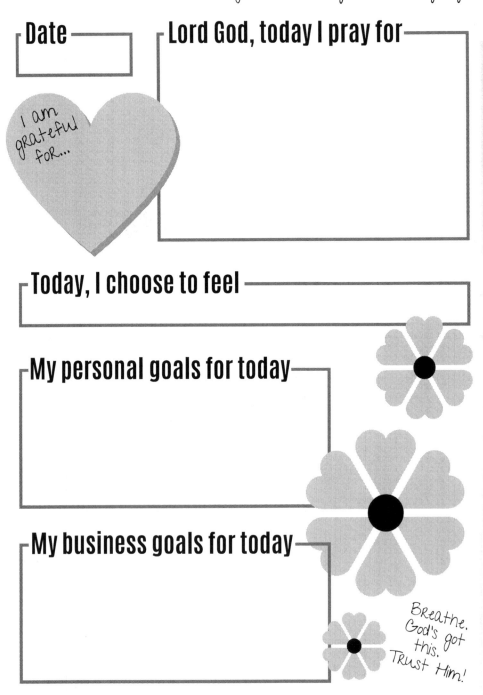

Date

I am grateful for...

Lord God, today I pray for

Today, I choose to feel

My personal goals for today

My business goals for today

Breathe. God's got this. Trust Him!

am grateful for a life full of God's infinite blessings. My heart is open to what's next. I trust Him.

Lord God, thank you for

my favorite moment/memory from today was

Today, I felt

I achieved my personal goals | Yes :: No
I achieved my business goals | Yes :: No

How and why was I successful in my daily goals? What needs to change?

Trust in God's timing. Relax. Breathe. Rest.

I am strong. I am brave. I am loved. I am favored. I welcome God's provision and guidance today, and everyday.

Date

Lord God, today I pray for

I am grateful for...

Today, I choose to feel

My personal goals for today

My business goals for today

Breathe. God's got this. Trust Him!

am grateful for a life full of God's infinite blessings. My heart is open to what's next. I trust Him.

Lord God, thank you for

my favorite moment/memory from today was

Today, I felt

I achieved my personal goals | Yes :: No
I achieved my business goals | Yes :: No

How and why was I successful in my daily goals? What needs to change?

Trust in God's timing. Relax. Breathe. Rest.

GOOD MORNING COURAGEOUS MAMA

I am strong. I am brave. I am loved. I am favored. I welcome God's provision and guidance today, and everyday.

Date

I am grateful for...

Lord God, today I pray for

Today, I choose to feel

My personal goals for today

My business goals for today

Breathe. God's got this. Trust Him!

am grateful for a life full of God's infinite blessings. My heart is open to what's next. I trust Him.

Lord God, thank you for

my favorite moment/memory from today was

Today, I felt

I achieved my personal goals | Yes :: No
I achieved my business goals | Yes :: No

How and why was I successful in my daily goals? What needs to change?

Trust in God's timing. Relax. Breathe. Rest.

I am strong. I am brave. I am loved. I am favored. I welcome God's provision and guidance today, and everyday.

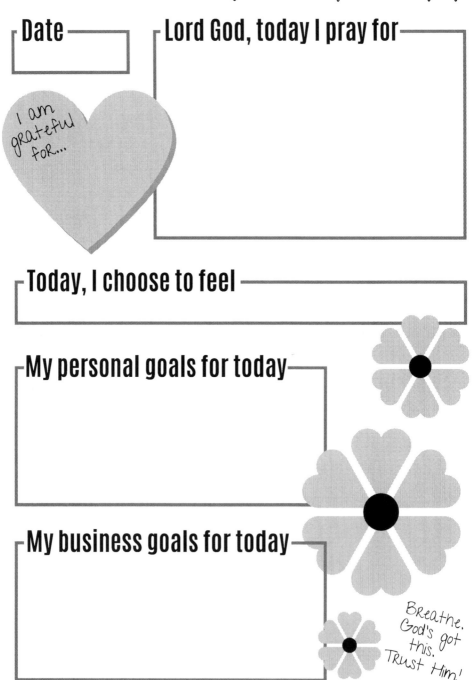

Date

Lord God, today I pray for

I am grateful for...

Today, I choose to feel

My personal goals for today

My business goals for today

Breathe. God's got this. Trust Him!

am grateful for a life full of God's infinite blessings. My heart is open to what's next. I trust Him.

Lord God, thank you for

my favorite moment/memory from today was

Today, I felt

I achieved my personal goals | Yes :: No
I achieved my business goals | Yes :: No

How and why was I successful in my daily goals? What needs to change?

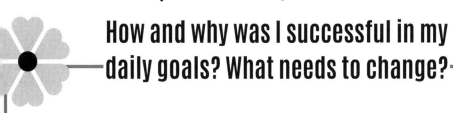

I Trust in God's timing. Relax. Breathe. Rest.

I am strong. I am brave. I am loved. I am favored. I welcome God's provision and guidance today, and everyday.

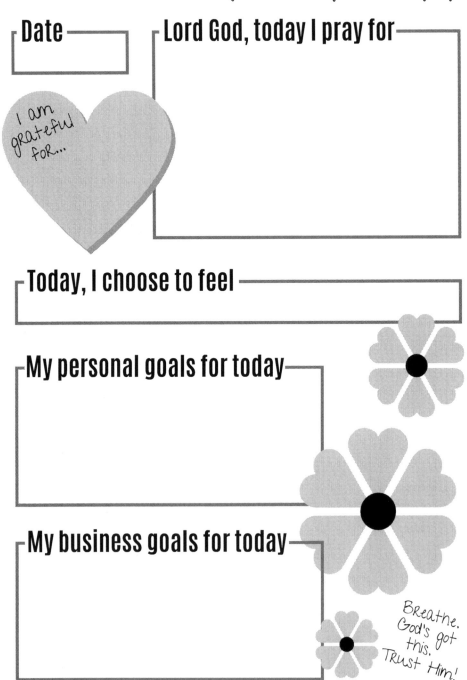

Date

Lord God, today I pray for

I am grateful for...

Today, I choose to feel

My personal goals for today

My business goals for today

Breathe. God's got this. Trust Him!

I am grateful for a life full of God's infinite blessings. My heart is open to what's next. I trust Him.

Lord God, thank you for

my favorite moment/memory from today was

Today, I felt

I achieved my personal goals **Yes :: No**
I achieved my business goals **Yes :: No**

How and why was I successful in my daily goals? What needs to change?

I trust in God's timing. Relax. Breathe. Rest.

I am strong. I am brave. I am loved. I am favored. I welcome God's provision and guidance today, and everyday.

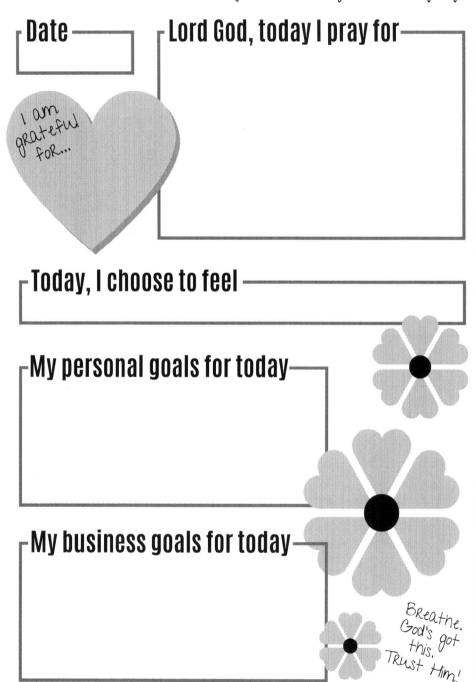

Date

Lord God, today I pray for

I am grateful for...

Today, I choose to feel

My personal goals for today

My business goals for today

Breathe. God's got this. Trust Him!

I am grateful for a life full of God's infinite blessings. My heart is open to what's next. I trust Him.

Lord God, thank you for

my favorite moment/memory from today was

Today, I felt

I achieved my personal goals — Yes :: No
I achieved my business goals — Yes :: No

How and why was I successful in my daily goals? What needs to change?

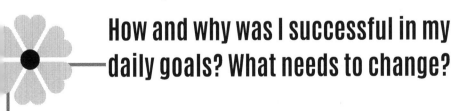

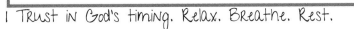
I trust in God's timing. Relax. Breathe. Rest.

I am stRoNg. I am bRave. I am loved. I am favoRed. I welcome God's pRovision and guidance today, and everyday.

Date

Lord God, today I pray for

I am gRateful foR...

Today, I choose to feel

My personal goals for today

My business goals for today

BReathe. God's got this. TRust Him!

I am grateful for a life full of God's infinite blessings. My heart is open to what's next. I trust Him.

Lord God, thank you for

my favorite moment/memory from today was

Today, I felt

I achieved my personal goals | Yes :: No
I achieved my business goals | Yes :: No

How and why was I successful in my daily goals? What needs to change?

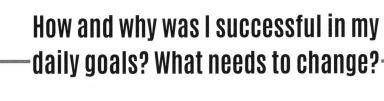

I Trust in God's timing. Relax. Breathe. Rest.

I am strong. I am brave. I am loved. I am favored. I welcome God's provision and guidance today, and everyday.

Date

Lord God, today I pray for

I am grateful for...

Today, I choose to feel

My personal goals for today

My business goals for today

Breathe. God's got this. Trust Him!

I am grateful for a life full of God's infinite blessings. My heart is open to what's next. I trust Him.

Lord God, thank you for

my favorite moment/memory from today was

Today, I felt

I achieved my personal goals   **Yes :: No**
I achieved my business goals   **Yes :: No**

How and why was I successful in my daily goals? What needs to change?

Trust in God's timing. Relax. Breathe. Rest.

I am strong. I am brave. I am loved. I am favored. I welcome God's provision and guidance today, and everyday.

Date

I am grateful for...

Lord God, today I pray for

Today, I choose to feel

My personal goals for today

My business goals for today

Breathe. God's got this. Trust Him!

am grateful for a life full of God's infinite blessings. My
heart is open to what's next. I trust Him.

Lord God, thank you for

my favorite
moment/memory
from today was

Today, I felt

I achieved my personal goals | Yes :: No
I achieved my business goals | Yes :: No

How and why was I successful in my
daily goals? What needs to change?

I Trust in God's timing. Relax. Breathe. Rest.

I am strong. I am brave. I am loved. I am favored. I welcome God's provision and guidance today, and everyday.

Date

Lord God, today I pray for

I am grateful for...

Today, I choose to feel

My personal goals for today

My business goals for today

Breathe. God's got this. Trust Him!

I am grateful for a life full of God's infinite blessings. My heart is open to what's next. I trust Him.

Lord God, thank you for

my favorite moment/memory from today was

Today, I felt

I achieved my personal goals | Yes :: No
I achieved my business goals | Yes :: No

How and why was I successful in my daily goals? What needs to change?

I Trust in God's timing. Relax. Breathe. Rest.

I am strong. I am brave. I am loved. I am favored. I welcome God's provision and guidance today, and everyday.

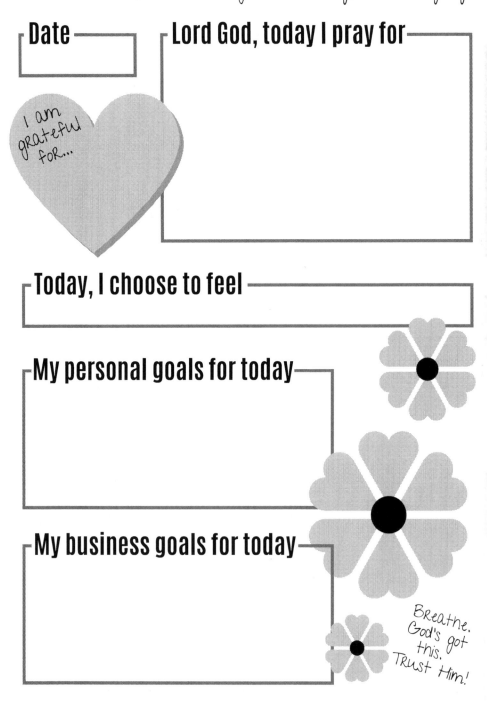

Date

Lord God, today I pray for

I am grateful for...

Today, I choose to feel

My personal goals for today

My business goals for today

Breathe. God's got this. Trust Him!

I am grateful for a life full of God's infinite blessings. My heart is open to what's next. I trust Him.

Lord God, thank you for

my favorite moment/memory from today was

Today, I felt

I achieved my personal goals | Yes :: No
I achieved my business goals | Yes :: No

How and why was I successful in my daily goals? What needs to change?

I Trust in God's timing. Relax. Breathe. Rest.

I am strong. I am brave. I am loved. I am favored. I welcome God's provision and guidance today, and everyday.

Date

Lord God, today I pray for

I am grateful for...

Today, I choose to feel

My personal goals for today

My business goals for today

Breathe. God's got this. Trust Him!

am grateful for a life full of God's infinite blessings. My heart is open to what's next. I trust Him.

Lord God, thank you for

my favorite moment/memory from today was

Today, I felt

I achieved my personal goals | Yes :: No
I achieved my business goals | Yes :: No

How and why was I successful in my daily goals? What needs to change?

I Trust in God's timing. Relax. Breathe. Rest.

I am strong. I am brave. I am loved. I am favored. I welcome God's provision and guidance today, and everyday.

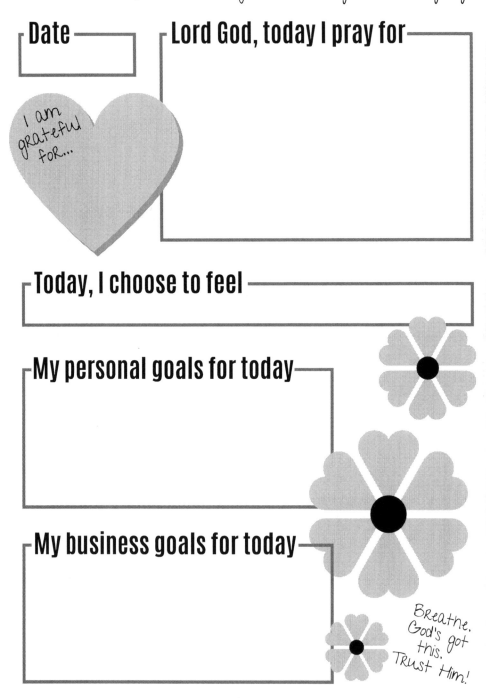

Date

Lord God, today I pray for

I am grateful for...

Today, I choose to feel

My personal goals for today

My business goals for today

Breathe. God's got this. Trust Him!

I am grateful for a life full of God's infinite blessings. My heart is open to what's next. I trust Him.

Lord God, thank you for

my favorite moment/memory from today was

Today, I felt

I achieved my personal goals | Yes :: No
I achieved my business goals | Yes :: No

How and why was I successful in my daily goals? What needs to change?

I trust in God's timing. Relax. Breathe. Rest.

Ideas :: Inspiration :: Notes

Ideas :: Inspiration :: Notes

Ideas :: Inspiration :: Notes

Ideas :: Inspiration :: Notes

Ideas :: Inspiration :: Notes

Ideas :: Inspiration :: Notes

Ideas :: Inspiration :: Notes

Ideas :: Inspiration :: Notes

Ideas :: Inspiration :: Notes

Ideas :: Inspiration :: Notes

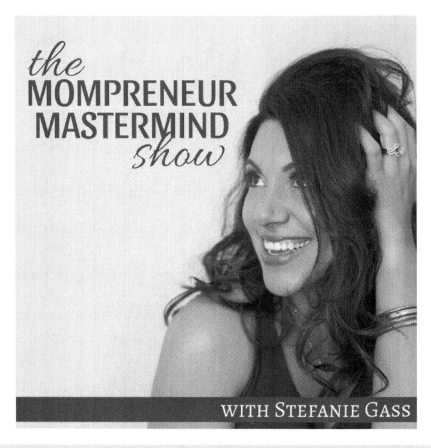

the
MOMPRENEUR
MASTERMIND
show

WITH STEFANIE GASS

Are You A Christ-Centered Entrepreneur?

Come subscribe to The Mompreneur Mastermind Show, Podcast!

Inspiring interviews, marketing, sales, balance, scaling your business, and stepping into your own potential!
bit.ly/themompreneurmastermindshow

Stefanie Gass helps mompreneurs create passive income businesses that light them up! Fueled by Jesus, iced coffee, & toddler snuggles, Stef is both an exceptional mama AND an extremely successful entrepreneur.

Stef's call is empowering women to claim their BEST lives by working less, yet making more.

Stef believes that when we let God's miracles light our path, we will profit from our passions, live proactively, & design a life that fuels our souls.

She believes we can actually have it all.

Let's Connect!

Podcast:
bit.ly/themompreneurmaster
mindshow

Website: stefaniegass.com
IG: @stefaniegass

FB Community:
bit.ly/successsupportgroup

support@stefaniegass.com

Made in the USA
Middletown, DE
02 August 2019